P9-DFT-671

ENDORSEMENTS

"*Three Hours to Live* is a book that will open your heart to the supernatural realm that God has made available to us. It will also soften your heart to the importance and power of prayer!"

—James Jones, MLB Player

"Jonathan Rizzo is a natural-born storyteller, and he tells his dramatic, life-changing tale compellingly in *Three Hours to Live*. The reader will not only be captivated by Jonathan's narrative, but will also come away with an appreciation for the uniqueness and value of their own story and a renewed passion to share it with someone else."

—Valerie Balcombe, Pastor's Wife, Miss Val, Teacher, Friend

"*Three Hours to Live* shows us that God can use anybody in His kingdom, whether experiencing the highs of life or the most extreme lows, to portray His mighty power, and to simply show us He is the true Living God. Jonathan Rizzo has blessed everyone reading this book by sharing his story of going through the eye of a hurricane and making it out with Jesus as the cornerstone of his story."

—Wes Horton, Carolina Panthers

"*Three Hours to Live* is an engaging story of how one man, Jonathan Rizzo, faced death and learned to live. It is an account of God's faithfulness, and how we too can turn our own stories into God's glories. It is a must-read!"

—Pastor Joe Houser, Lead Pastor of OB One Church

"Jonathan's personal story through the valley of death, back to life, and the earthly struggles that followed, is a harrowing journey through the unknown. In one of the most humble and energetic stories you will ever read, Jonathan opens his heart and his life to his readers and begs us to turn to Jesus."

—Wade LeBlanc, MLB Player

three
HOURS
TO LIVE

JONATHAN RIZZO

Three Hours to Live
Copyright © 2018 by Jonathan Rizzo

All rights reserved. Printed in the United States of America. No part of this book may be used or reproduced in any manner whatsoever without written permission except in the case of brief quotations embodied in critical articles or reviews.

Scripture quotations marked (NIV) are taken from the Holy Bible, New International Version®, NIV®. Copyright © 1973, 1978, 1984, 2011 by Biblica, Inc.™ Used by permission of Zondervan. All rights reserved worldwide. www.zondervan.com The "NIV" and "New International Version" are trademarks registered in the United States Patent and Trademark Office by Biblica, Inc.™

ISBN: 978-0-578-20680-6 paperback

For More Information:
www.jonathanrizzo.org

Or Contact via Email:
threehourstolive@gmail.com

To Grandma Rizzo,
who went to be with Jesus right before this book went to print.
I love and miss you.

FOREWORD

I give myself one patient a year to get invested in. That's not to say that I don't attempt to bring one hundred percent of my professional abilities with me every day I come to work. It means that as an ICU nurse, I have had to develop a hard outer shell. The stories of my patients can be truly tragic and heartbreaking, and they will take every piece of you with them, if you allow it.

Being ill is a part of the human condition. That's something you get used to. Being present at the end of a life well-lived in a way that is dignified, meaningful and pain-free—that, you get used to. But looking at people younger than you who are sicker than they have any right to be, who have yet to experience so many things and share their talents with the world: that, you never get used to. I don't care who you are, that hurts. I've been a nurse since the late 1990s. I've worked in Trauma and Transplant and ICU, and no matter who or when, it always hurts when you lose someone.

I came to know God a bit on the later side. Religion wasn't part of my childhood, despite my couple of years in parochial school. It definitely wasn't part of college. But after a separation and subsequent divorce in 2006, I wanted more: Community, morals, just more. At a friend's suggestion, I visited a few churches and attended each at least twice. I hit gold on my second church, though I played around a bit longer. When I finally came back, I looked around and saw emotions I had yet to feel but literally pined for. I saw one hundred percent genuine joy and zero percent obligation. I saw home.

Years went by and my view on my patients and my patients' families changed as I met more people and progressed in my Christian walk. I worked full time and attended at least one small home group and two services a week. I didn't care that I'd hear the same message twice in a weekend; I just wanted to grow and know more. I pestered people I admired to learn more about being better than myself. Had I known Jonathan in these early days, I'd likely have pestered him too.

I still kept my emotional reserve at work as much as possible. Still raw from the divorce, worried about my father far away, and being the mother of a precocious ball of energy, I just didn't have it to spare. Clinicians have a special kind of multiple personality disorder; whatever's happening outside, we still work hard to set our faces, click our pens and tuck our stethoscopes around our necks. We're still human, so I admit outside life leaks through more than most of us would like. We check the chart, check the patients, and check the boxes. There's so much to be done in a finite and regulated time, we tend to also check our emotions at the door. We make the right noises and murmurs, we educate and advocate, but it's with a degree or two of separation.

Most of the time.

When Jonathan came along, he scared a lot of us. He was so sick. Laypeople may not know this, but when an ICU nurse says someone is that sick, we're already mentally reviewing the contents of the crash cart and looking around for who will likely jump into the fray with us. When Jonathan came in, we had been through October's flu wave, with all the associated H1N1 hysteria, largely unruffled.

However, it was like the first wave was a diversion. The following July landed us in absolutely the most brutal flu season I've witnessed. Influenza is such a hard target to hit; seasonal vaccines are a very educated, scrutinized guess, and some years' vaccines are more on target than others. Usually the very young or very old are most at risk, and typically adults have a few days or weeks of manageable misery. The 2009 H1N1 strain, the strain that got Jonathan, was different. It moved with a speed and ferocity I'd not really seen just a few months earlier. I mean, this flu killed with all the finesse of a bull in a china shop. It didn't just keep you on the couch for a couple of days; it laid you out within hours, taking your respiratory and renal systems with it. As bizarre as it seems, it had a special predilection for people in the middle years; it hunted the college students and mothers, but not babies or grandmothers. Influenza vaccine development and production is a lengthy process, and an FDA-approved H1N1 vaccine wasn't available until September 2009.

When Jonathan arrived to the ICU, I was assigned to different patients down the hall. I saw a bunch of activity and kind of dismissed it at first. Patients come in extremis all the time-it's the ICU. But the whole unit's mood changed when the doctor made the proclamation that Jonathan would need a proning bed. This bed is huge. I mean, Michael Bay-ridiculous huge. That meant a transfer to a larger room down the hall, a transfer from bed to bed, and then initiation of the proning therapy.

Proning therapy is no joke. As Jonathan was wheeled by in the standard ICU bed, I thought he was too far gone. My first thought was, "Oh my God, they're going to flip him and he's going to code." But to my relief, he did well when prone. Less well when supine (on his back). This is common in patients with significant, usually devastating lung injury. Praise be to God, my initial thoughts never came to fruition.

Over the next couple of weeks, I came to know his family and friends. I saw the multitude of pictures on the counter in the room; celebrities, friends, family. You could just tell this kid was someone people enjoyed being around, even though I hadn't met him. You can't know someone by the periphery, not really. But despite that, my heart just filled more and more each time he was in my assignment. I'd watch his mom, Teresa, sit vigilantly around the clock, the worry lines deepen on his dad, Dan's, face, and the blatant hope and pleading on the faces of his friends and little brother, Alex. I'd watch Teresa journal, doze and talk with the doctors while dealing with her own health issues. I came to deeply admire how well she balanced it all, never breaking. She was Jonathan's warrior, and it broke my heart and fed my mama-soul all at once.

One of the most striking memories I have, second only to the memory of how ashen and ill he appeared rolling by the first time, is that it was just a "regular" day in the ICU. I'd gotten the shift report, an update on his progress the night before, and was on my way in to do my initial assessment and give morning medications. I saw Teresa in the corner, exhausted. I saw the pictures on the counter, all these smiling faces; and I saw Jonathan, so small compared to the monster bed. In that moment, I thought "Not this one. Just not this one. He's too young; he's a youth pastor. God, please, just not this one."

Well, wouldn't you know it, it wasn't this one. Not this time. After an initial couple of weeks of absolute extremes, he rallied and he rallied fast. Faster than I've seen anyone, really. And once he woke up, once he was off the bed and the ventilator and the dialysis machines and sedation and all the trappings of the fine line between here and Heaven, he was just the most amazing person. I finally got to "meet" him and really see why people are so drawn to him.

It took awhile for him to clear out the medications we'd used to keep him calm, asleep, out of pain, and it affected his memory. He couldn't yet talk, but he very quickly started to write. Every single time I went into the room, whether summoned or routine, he'd apologize. For what, I still don't know. More than once I'd reassure him and then step out for just a second to breathe and not cry. He was so small, so weak, he had every right to be fidgety or cranky or withdrawn. But he was none of those, and he was sorry!

Soon after that, his head cleared, the breathing tube came out, and he was discharged out of the ICU. Very quickly after that, out of the hospital. His turnaround was as sudden and unexpected as his decline, and I believed then as I do now: all that prayer, his warrior mom, his God-chosen need to be around-it all worked. God's choices, His timing, His provisions aren't always immediately apparent, but Jonathan's recovery absolutely cemented my belief that God had gone before all of us. He had cleared the way, and none of us would want to know what it would look like if He hadn't gone on ahead. All we have to do is take steps in His direction. We'll get there, to where He's already provided a place, with

Him both in front encouraging us forward and beside, whispering, "I'm still here. I've never left you."

I'm so glad God did what He did. He started working on my Miracle Man in front of me, and unbeknownst to me, still continued working on my own heart and faith in the process. But years before, He called me, He broke me, and only then did He allow me to witness something incredible.

ICU nurses don't often get to see the fruits of their labors. We admit, treat and transfer. We hope for the best, pretty certain the best isn't always the likely result. It's so rare and so special to see somebody you didn't think would survive the next few hours to not just survive, but thrive. Jonathan worked his way back literally from the brink, leaving almost half the man he was when he showed up at our door. He has become a husband, father, supporter, pastor, author—so many things. Had God not called me when He did and given all those years in between to make me ready, I would've missed it. And that would be something I could never get used to.

For all the terrifying moments, there have been double the victories and I'm changed and humbled to have been a part. Thank you, Jonathan, for being exceptional in so many ways.

—Rachel Cook, one of Jonathan's ICU nurses

introduction

THREE HOURS TO LIVE.
SPOILER ALERT: I LIVED.

Hi, I'm Jonathan. Maybe we've met before—maybe you've heard me speak in person or on the radio. Maybe you found this book online or happened upon it in your local bookstore. Maybe a friend, neighbor or family member gave you this book as a gift. However you came across it, I'm so excited *you* are reading *Three Hours to Live*! Thanks for allowing me to share my story with you. I hope you will enjoy it.

When I read, I always imagine myself in the story I'm reading. I like to close my eyes and put myself in the situation that is presented before me. I visualize every detail. The setting. My surroundings. The colors. The noises. This allows me to stay more engaged. My hope is that when you read my story, you are able to do the same. I want you to put yourself in my position when you read this book. I want you to close your eyes and imagine all the sights and sounds—all the details that make this story become real. I truly want you to grasp the power of Jesus.

Do you have a bucket list? You know, that list of things you want to do before you die? My bucket list is pretty long. I want to travel to all fifty states. I want to run a full marathon. I want to spend two straight weeks of my life lying in a hammock over the water in the Maldives. I want to see a baseball game in every stadium. I want a signed Mike Trout bat to hang on my wall. I want to take batting practice with the players at Petco Park. I want to be a guest on *The Tonight Show* with Jimmy Fallon. And those are just a few of the things on my list.

I've already checked a bunch of other things off my bucket list: I've been skydiving, I've been a contestant on *The Price Is Right* and won a lot of fun prizes. That one was on my list because my one-hundred-two-year-old Grandma Vera watched that show every morning. She freaked out when she saw me on stage.

Something else that had always been on my list was writing a book. I wasn't sure this was a list item I'd be able to check off. I mean, seriously, I was a typical twenty-four-year-old guy. What did I have to write a book about? Who would read it? The answer to that question was no one! But I kept it on my bucket list. I always thought it would be so rad to sit at a table at a local bookstore and sign a book with my name on it. Not for the fame or the glory, but just to have accomplished such a difficult task.

But understand this book is not simply a checkmark on my bucket list. I'm not writing this just to say I've done it. I'm writing this because, back when I was twenty-four, almost twenty-five, something crazy happened to me. The answer to the question, "What would I have to write a book about?" suddenly became clear in a way I never could have predicted and didn't particularly want.

Over the next several chapters we'll spend together, the *why* of this book will come into focus. You'll read about how I was living life as a very regular guy—in a relationship, sharing a condo with one of my best friends, working in corporate America, just hired on as a part-time youth pastor. And you'll read about how everything turned upside down overnight.

My prayer is that when you put this book down, you will know that you are loved by God and that you have been created for a mighty purpose. My desire is that this book gives you hope and a renewed passion for Jesus Christ. This book is for everyone—young, old, believer and nonbeliever. It truly doesn't matter who you are or where you come from—I'm writing this story for you.

I'm going to keep it real. There is no sugar-coating with me, in real life or on these pages. I say it how it is. But also know that every word in this book has been prayed over. Every person reading this book has been prayed for. I've prayed for you to be touched, to be changed.

This is my story, to the best of my recollection. I have asked those who witnessed my nightmare and lived it alongside me to fill in the missing pieces. Thank you for taking this journey with me. Be blessed. Be happy. Be encouraged.

I love you.

one

GASPING

It's three a.m., July 26, 2009, and I can't breathe.

Why can't I breathe?

I struggled out of bed and stumbled down the hall to the bathroom. Placing both hands on the counter, I leaned over the sink and began coughing up blood. A lot of blood. The sounds of my coughing and the light from the bathroom woke up my mom.

"Jonathan? Jonathan!" she yelled. "Are you okay?"

Struggling through the blood, I rasped, "Mom, I'm spitting up blood and can barely breathe."

She and my dad appeared in the bathroom in seconds. "Put your clothes on," my mom said immediately. "We're going to the hospital."

"You stay, Teresa," my dad said. "I'll take him." My little brother Alex was at a church camp, and my mom would need to pick him up in the late morning. Dad said, "They will probably just hook Jonathan up to some IVs, and we'll be back in a few hours."

That made sense to all of us at the time. Looking back now, we can see the warning signs leading up to that moment. Looking back, we can see there were clues to how serious my condition was about to become. In that moment, it seemed perfectly reasonable to assume that when we got to the E.R., they would simply hook me up to an IV to rehydrate me. I'd been sick all week, but...people get sick all the time. How often is it life-threatening?

One week earlier, the previous Sunday, I played a softball game and then went to my friend Jeff's house for dinner. I drove myself there. I really wasn't feeling well, but this dinner had been planned for a few weeks, and I didn't want to cancel.

After dinner, I drove straight to the emergency room. It turned out my temperature was over 104 degrees—dangerously high. My body was weak, and I was absolutely exhausted, but I didn't know why. At the hospital, they did a spinal tap for meningitis, which turned out to be negative. They hooked me up to IVs because I was dehydrated. The doctors did a chest x-ray to check for pneumonia, and the results came back completely clear. So I felt terrible, but nothing really seemed to be wrong with me.

I was released at six the next morning, and returned to the condo I shared with my friend Andy in the Mission Valley area of San Diego. We had just moved in a few weeks prior.

Even though they had released me from the E.R. and all the tests had been negative, I literally couldn't get off the couch. I had no energy and was still battling a ridiculously high fever. I took the entire week off work, which was something I rarely did. It showed just how bad I felt.

My entire body ached. I was sweating and hot. It felt like a train had hit me. I had never experienced anything like this before. Andy was waiting on me with soup and light snack food, because that was all I wouldn't throw up.

Two days later, my sister, Sara, called to ask how I was doing. I told her I was not well, and she decided to come down and bring me some soup for lunch. When she got there, she saw in person how terrible I was. I barely had enough strength to sit up. After she left, she called my mom to tell her how weak I was getting. I had a skull-splitting headache, and even though I was still sweating, I now felt very cold. My dad, Dan, came down later that day and picked me up so I could rest at my parents' house. He helped me walk down the steps, where he opened the door to his truck and put me inside.

The drive to Ramona, the town where I grew up, was about forty minutes, and the motion made me even more miserable. We got to their house and I immediately collapsed into the bed in my sister's old room. I had no strength to move.

My mother noticed I had already lost some weight and she monitored me closely. Although I was at my parents' house being cared for by my "nurse" mom, I didn't feel any better. I couldn't understand why the over-the-counter medication was not improving my condition. I was missing work and couldn't wait to get healthy again. As each day passed, I knew I was not getting any better.

In fact, I was getting weaker.

On Friday, July 24, my mom took me to our family doctor, who diagnosed me with the flu, bronchitis, and possibly pneumonia. He put me on a Z-Pack and told me to rest and drink plenty of fluids, and sent me home. I felt more miserable, weaker, and more exhausted than the previous days.

On Saturday night, my then-girlfriend came over and we watched a movie. I ate an egg for dinner and was feeling better than I had all week. This was a big deal because I had not eaten anything for several days. I went to bed around eleven that night, hoping that when I awakened, this nightmare would be over. Little did I know this nightmare was just beginning. Hours later, I was spitting blood into the sink.

Deep coughing shook my body, and it was becoming more and more difficult to breathe. My father helped me to the car once again, and we rushed down to the emergency room. It was still very early in the morning and pitch-black outside. Very few cars were out on the road as we drove to Sharp Grossmont Hospital. We arrived Sunday morning around 4:30.

My dad dropped me off in the circle in front of the double glass sliding doors, and he went to park the car. I walked myself into the crowded E.R. and checked in. It took all my strength just to fill out the forms and give them my insurance information. I grabbed the closest chair and fell into it. I was so cold waiting for my dad to join me. By the time he got in, I could barely hold my head up. I was gasping for every breath of air. The heaving of my chest alerted the nurses that something was seriously wrong.

I was hurried back into a small, very dark room filled with machines where a nurse took my temperature as I tried to focus on the machines surrounding me. The room was fuzzy, and I felt like I was slipping in and out of consciousness. I was still very cold and gasping for breath. I noticed the worried look on my dad's face. Fear pulsed through me.

One of the E.R. nurses, Laila, happened to arrive to work early that day. She was a former ICU nurse, and when she saw me, she knew something was very wrong. She rushed to the admitting doctor, Dr. Fox, whom she happened to be dating, and asked him to see me immediately.

Dr. Fox examined me and agreed with Laila: my condition was extremely critical. He ordered tests to be taken immediately, and knowing I would be headed to the ICU, Laila hand-picked the best of the best nurses to oversee my care. As Dr. Fox said later, from the moment I arrived in the emergency room, Laila hovered over me like a bird over her egg. She knew that every minute was critical.

They put me in a bed right away. Three hospital staffers quickly converged on me, running around my room performing various tests. A nurse was taking my pulse, a technologist set up a chest x-ray, and a phlebotomist drew blood. A respiratory therapist entered the room and swabbed my mouth and nose. It was all happening so fast. My dad was in the corner, concern lining his face. I couldn't remember ever seeing him look so intense.

I watched their urgency with confusion. Why were there so many nurses and technologists entering and exiting my room? What were they testing me for? They didn't bother to tell me what was going on and I didn't want to slow them down with my questions. Although I did not understand the doctor's lingo, the vibe everyone put off was very solemn. My dad listened intently, but neither one of us knew what was going on.

We had expected some IV fluids. We had expected to be discharged back to Ramona fairly quickly. We had not expected…this.

Hurrying through their tests, the medical staff scurried about me, talking in short, covert phrases with an unmistakable sense of urgency. Nurses were breezing in and out through the room, like angels flying in and out of Heaven, assisting the technicians with their tests.

The nurses hooked me up to an IV and hung it from a stand. After a few moments, Dr. Fox came up to my dad and looked him in the eyes. "His blood oxygen levels are declining as each minute passes. If this were my son, I'd be scared shi*less." When I share my story, I always share this exact phrase the doctor used, because even I know that doctors don't usually offer personal opinions or swear when talking to patients' families. It points out the seriousness of the situation I was in. The doctor was keeping it as real as he could so my dad would understand just how serious my illness was.

A maze of tubes and flashing machines were hooked up to me. Surrounded by bright lights and beeping signals, I showed a steady and continual decline. My life was slipping away. I began hyperventilating, gasping to change my fate.

Dr. Fox yelled orders at the other medical staff. Then he turned to my dad. "Your son has three hours to live!"

two

DEATH'S DOOR

I played sports throughout my entire childhood and adolescence. I played soccer and baseball for fourteen years and volleyball all four years of high school. I was also a drummer in a band for four years. I had lifted weights regularly for the six years leading up to this terrible morning. I was twenty-four years old, 210 pounds of muscle with a body fat percentage of less than ten. I was in peak physical condition.

So the very last thing my dad or I expected to hear was that I was about to die.

"You're not going to remember the next few days," Dr. Fox said amidst the chaos.

I wondered what he meant by that, but he'd already left my side, too busy for me to ask any questions.

I lay there, staring at my shoes—white with black stripes. Then I pulled my cell phone out of the pocket of my shorts and called my girlfriend. It was around 4:50 in the morning, and I woke her up from a deep sleep. I was barely able to whisper, "I'm at the hospital. I'm not going to be able to talk for a few days. I love—"

"Get off the phone!" Dr. Fox shouted as he ran into the room. "Off the phone. We have work to do." The urgency in his voice clearly indicated the severity of my illness, even in my confusion.

Terror seized me, and I handed my cell phone over to my father. Blank and numb with shock, he finished the conversation with my girlfriend, told her what was going on, then quickly hung up.

Dr. Fox ordered me to lie completely flat and told my father to leave the room. As soon as my dad shut the door behind himself, he heard the doctors yelling at me. "Open your mouth! Open your mouth!"

My dad took one step into the hallway and called my mom. "Teresa, you need to get to the hospital right away. It isn't looking good for our son."

My mom rushed out the door and drove the forty-five minutes to the hospital. I imagine those were the longest forty-five minutes of her life, not knowing if her son would be alive when she made it to the E.R.

On the drive down, she called one of our closest family friends, Jan Brown. Jan worked at a church in Ramona, and she started a prayer chain. As the sun was rising, most of the churches in Ramona had gotten the emergency prayer request for me. By the time services started later that morning, thousands of prayer warriors from all over town were lifting me up in prayer from the pulpit and in congregations.

I don't recall the doctor shouting at me to open my mouth. How my mouth got open, I don't know. At that moment, I could only think about one thing: I knew beyond a shadow of a doubt that death was knocking on my door.

It was like being in a movie. You know those moments where chaos is swirling around, and you're seeing it all from one character's perspective? Then suddenly everything slows down to super slow-motion and all goes silent. That's what it felt like. Everything slowed. Everything quieted.

"And the peace of God, which transcends all understanding, will guard your hearts and your minds in Christ Jesus."

—Philippians 4:7

I closed my eyes, folded my arms, and prayed, "Lord, if this is it, I am ready to go home. This is why we live—to go home. Please forgive me for all my sins." I didn't *want* to die because I was only twenty-four years old. I had a lot of goals and unfulfilled plans for my life. Remember that long bucket list? Not only were most of my bucket list items still undone, I always knew I wanted to be a husband and a dad. None of my plans would come true if I were to die on that bed, so I continued praying, "I don't want to die, but if this is Your will, I'm ready to go home. Amen."

Despite the hectic buzzing around me, and the loud, flashing monitors, I couldn't hear a thing. The greatest peace I have ever experienced in my life settled over me. I knew this peace came from the Lord Jesus Christ. At that very moment, I was ready to die, if that was God's will.

A moment later, I slipped into a coma.

three

COMATOSE

The coma wasn't an accident. The doctors determined the only chance I had at survival was to put me into a drug-induced coma until they could figure out what was killing me. At the time they filled my IV with the sedation drugs, they didn't even have a guess at what was wrong with me.

My blood oxygen saturation percentage was 47 and falling fast. Normal blood oxygen saturation levels are around 95% to 99%, with 100% being ideal. When levels dip below 50%, you are at extreme risk of death. If you survive, there's a strong chance you'll have serious brain damage. The lack of oxygen to the brain shuts it down. The doctors and nurses were concerned that would be my fate.

They administered a paralytic drug so that I wouldn't pull out my tubes and to put less stress on my body. Even in a coma, a person's natural reaction is to pull out their tubes. And I had a lot of them: the breathing tube that went through my mouth to help me breathe, IVs large and small, a feeding tube that traveled from my nose directly to my stomach, and that wretched tube that continuously drained my bladder. I needed the breathing tube and its attached ventilator, with all the awful accessories that accompanied it. My lungs weren't functioning; they were incapable of providing my body with the oxygen it needed.

The doctors were administering antibiotics, rehydration fluids, medications to keep my blood pressure up, pain medication like morphine, and sedatives and paralytics to make sure my body was calm and at rest. But they were only beginning to guess what was wrong with me.

They met with my parents to tell them I would not live through the night.

My mom called my older brother, Daniel, right away and told him to fly to California as soon as he could. He lived in Ohio at the time, but he dropped everything and made it out that evening. Daniel is a surgeon. When he got to the hospital, he saw my vitals and spoke to the doctors in the technical terms only medical professionals fully understand so that he could try to translate for my family. He came out of my room, looked at our parents, and said, "I don't think he is going to make it."

My family sat together and prayed. There was nothing else they could do.

By the grace of God, I made it through the night. But before anyone could take a moment to be relieved, most of my internal organs shut down.

My vitals crashed, and the crew of doctors rushed in. Desperately, they tried to pull me back from death's grip. I was never pronounced dead, but I was basically lifeless. I was as close to death as you can possibly get without actually dying.

They stabilized my vitals and decided on a Hail Mary move to try to save me. It was Nurse Laila's idea. She suggested a pronation bed. A pronation bed costs hundreds of thousands of dollars and is only used in the most extreme circumstances. Although Sharp Grossmont Hospital had access to the bed, they hadn't used it in several years. Many on the hospital staff were surprised to discover that they still had a contract for this monster of a bed. That was a miracle in itself. Laila was familiar with these beds from her time in ICU, and she thought it might be my only chance.

The best way to describe this piece of medical equipment is that it's like a giant rotisserie. You know, those metal rods at the grocery store delis where they place a whole chicken to rotate over an open flame? That's what a pronation bed does, except it flips 180 degrees back and forth instead of 360 degrees around. I was the chicken and the bed was the metal rod.

I desperately needed to start rotating so the fluid in my lungs would slosh around enough to transfer oxygen to my brain. My lungs had 70% pneumonia on both sides. They were flooded. I needed to rotate back and forth if I had any hope of preventing brain damage and saving my organs—and ultimately my life.

But many on the hospital staff wondered if I'd live long enough for the bed to be installed in my room. It took a day to order this specialty bed. They rushed as much as they were able. The bed finally arrived and the nurses strapped me into it. All you could see were my kneecaps, nose and toes. It truly looked like something out of NASA, a deep-space contraption for someone journeying to the other side of the universe.

And really, that notion wasn't far off from reality.

Several of the nurses had never seen this bed. It was so large that I had the biggest ICU room in the entire hospital. I'm claustrophobic, so it was a blessing from God that I had those coma-inducing drugs and paralytics in my system. If I had woken up, I would have freaked out.

I flipped 180 degrees back and forth constantly, and every four hours, the nurses would open the bed to change me, and make sure I was comfortable.

My kidneys weren't functioning, so I was hooked up to a dialysis machine, which ran continually. Most people on hemodialysis have a three-hour treatment three times a week. My blood pressure and breathing were so unstable; I couldn't tolerate the regular kind of dialysis. Instead, the machine ran continuously, twenty-four hours a day, stopping only if the filter needed to be changed.

Chest x-rays came back solid white from the pneumonia. My other organs had surrendered to the silent enemy invading my body.

The Sunday I was admitted to the hospital, my good friend and brother in Christ, Mark De La Cruz, created a website for everyone to follow and get updates about my condition. He posted photos, too, and there was a section where people could leave messages and notes of encouragement or support. Any time there was an update on me, or any time there was a specific or urgent prayer request, he would update the website. To this day, I visit the site once or twice a month, just to remember what the Lord has brought me through.

Thousands of people were praying for me in those crucial moments. I made it through another night—three hours to live and holding. It can only be because of those many prayers offered to God on my behalf. There's no medical reason why I survived that day. The next day they evaluated me and met with my family again.

After the doctors talked to my family, this was the update Mark posted to the website: "No change in his condition. The doctors say the goal for the next few days is stability. The family has been told not to expect any improvement for a while and that they may see more episodes like yesterday where things may take a turn for the worse. Pray for stability, for improvement (even though it is not expected) and for the doctors to find the root cause of this."

My mother also kept a diary while I was in the hospital. She wrote in it every day. On this particular day she wrote to me in her diary: "It is so hard sitting here not knowing if you'll be okay. We just have to trust Jesus. He knows best. Even your doctor, Dr. Al Naser, said there's only so much the doctors can do. The rest is in the hands of the Lord Jesus."

Hearing Dr. Al Naser say that he believed that they were doing all they could was comforting to her, but the balance of my life was truly in the hands of the Lord, live or die.

In the Intensive Care Unit, the normal ratio is one nurse for every two patients. I was so critical that I had two nurses watching me around the clock. I had nineteen tubes and lines going into my body to keep me alive. At one point, my body temperature dropped so low that they had to get special blankets to blow warm air into my bed. They wrapped my body in these blankets to get my temperature back to normal.

Finally, the preliminary tests came back, and my silent killer was unmasked: H1N1, better known as Swine Flu.

four

MIRACLE MAN

To everyone's surprise, I made it through a few more days. As those days passed, some parts of my body would improve, but others would get worse. It was one step forward, two steps back.

My family and friends had camped out in the waiting room while I flipped lifelessly in the pronation bed for a week. People visited often, and many prayers were offered to the Lord Jesus Christ on my behalf. People brought home-cooked meals for my family, who were basically living in the hospital. A home-cooked meal was a welcome treat for the watchmen gathered on my behalf.

I slowly stabilized through that first week. My family needed a breath of fresh air and a change of scenery. They decided to walk across the street to a restaurant to get some dinner.

My mom wrote in her diary: "We had just ordered our food when we got a call from the hospital that you were awake and very restless. You were actually flipping out. They were proning you and since you were more awake now; you knew what was going on. The nurse asked for us to come right away. Since we had walked to the restaurant, dad and I had to run back to the hospital. We stayed with you for a long time. As long as you could see my face, you were fine. You were prone, face down, so I had to lie on my back, under your bed, so that you could see me."

If my mother hadn't written about this in her diary, I wouldn't know about it. I don't remember, thank God. Even though I was more awake, and the medication was wearing off, I have no memory of this freak-out. I am so thankful for this. It sounds like it would have been pretty traumatic.

At the time of my freak-out, I was on sixteen different medications, and the medical staff was manually removing fluid from my lungs. As the days went on, I would show some slight signs of improvement, and that would give my family, friends and the doctors a glimmer of hope. I was nowhere out of the woods yet, but they clung to any little shred of positivity. When they hadn't expected me to live past a few hours, a whole week of life was an inexplicable miracle.

And I didn't only last a week. Three hours to live, and still holding on. After two weeks, they decided I could be moved from the pronation bed to a transitional bed, which produced side-to-side motion, like a ship rocking back and forth. The fluid in my lungs still needed to be sloshed around. The transition bed was rather large, and although it did not flip upside down like the pronation bed, it moved my body from left to right, and then back again to continue to allow the air to escape from the fluid in my lungs and get to my organs. During this whole time, I was still technically in a coma. I have no memory of being in this bed but have gotten this account from my sister, who remembers it well.

If the doctors were only battling my organ failure and H1N1 infection, that would have kept them busy enough. But other ailments kept cropping up, and they were hitting me hard. I developed a nasty blood clot in my right calf, so I was put on a blood thinner.

On August 6, twelve days after I had been admitted, I had a blood transfusion with two units of blood. Two days later, I had another transfusion with two more units of blood. In all, I would have six total units of blood.

A few days later, I had a tracheostomy. The tube they had originally inserted into my airway was vital—I needed it to breathe. This type of tube went from my mouth to my lungs and was connected to the ventilator to help me breathe, but the balloon that encircles the outside of this breathing tube can cause damage to the windpipe if left in for too long. Having the tracheostomy gave my trachea a chance to heal while still allowing me to be on the ventilator with reliable airway access. Unfortunately, the blood thinner I had been placed on for my blood clot caused excessive bleeding during this surgery. Every fire the doctors extinguished in one part of my body ignited a new one somewhere else.

But the doctors didn't give up.

I remember coming out of the coma on August 13, after being comatose for nineteen days. I opened my eyes, and my gaze locked on a TV that was hanging on the wall in front of me in this very large, cold ICU room. I turned my head to the right and noticed my arm—how small it had become. It probably seems like a silly thought to have in that moment, but that is exactly what came to my mind. After not using a single muscle and living off liquids through tubes in your nose for nineteen days straight, you lose weight.

And I was rail thin. I entered the hospital weighing 210 pounds, and I left weighing 168 pounds. I lost forty-two pounds in the month I was in the hospital.

That was the first thing I noticed when I woke up; all my muscle was gone.

As my eyes continued to move, I noticed the nineteen lines and tubes that were connected to machines on one side and me on the other. With all the strength I had, I lifted the blanket off of my chest and saw the catheter that was connected to me.

I looked to my left and there was my mom, sitting in a chair, roughly two feet away from my bed. She was sitting upright, her legs crossed, and she was reading a magazine.

She glanced at me, and our eyes met. She took off her glasses and leaned toward me. Her voice was calm. "Hi, honey."

I couldn't make sense of anything I was seeing. My mind grasped for an explanation. The last thing that I remembered hearing prior to this was that I had three hours to live. Shouldn't I be dead now? I thought maybe

I was in Heaven. I also thought my mom had died and gone to Heaven with me.

But this was not Heaven. This was far from Heaven. There was pain, confusion, weakness, uncertainty. I quickly realized I was living a nightmare. I wanted to talk—to say something, anything—but I couldn't. I was still groggy. I tried to wrap my head around the fact that I was still in the hospital.

The next day I had an upper endoscopy procedure to check out my insides. I'd had several bronchoscopies while in the coma, as well as multiple surgeries. It was so weird not to be able to remember anything about them. But that same day, August 14, I was taken off of dialysis because my kidneys were working again. Praise God!

More than three weeks had passed since I'd even sat up in bed. The doctors said it was time to start therapy, even with many of my lines and machines still hooked up. It took a lot of effort—and a lot of help—to get into a seated position. I sat there for twenty-five minutes, and that was harder than many workouts I've done in the gym. My muscles, idle so long while I was in the coma, had atrophied.

When we progressed to standing, I couldn't believe how wobbly I was. I slouched over beside my bed, sure I'd do a faceplant at any moment. But the nurses encouraged me. They said I was improving faster than anyone they'd seen. Still... barely able to support myself, puffing with exertion when I wasn't even moving, I didn't see how that could be true.

Even though the medical staff was pleased with my progress, the doctor told me I would be in the hospital for another month and would not be home for my twenty-fifth birthday on September 15. Even if I had managed to get discharged from the hospital, the doctors told me I wouldn't be going home. I'd be going to a recovery facility to continue my physical therapy for an additional six months.

Six months.

That news was devastating. So, at that moment, I spoke truth into my life. I told myself that I would do everything I could to get out of the hospital as quickly as possible, and that I would go *home*, not to some therapy center. So I pushed myself—hard.

The ten days following my awakening, August 15 to 24, were filled with miracles. Miracles my doctors didn't expect and couldn't explain. The pneumonia vanished. For the first time in a month, I could breathe on my own with the help of an oxygen tank. I had two bites of applesauce. It doesn't sound like a big deal, but it was. And finally, my brain and mouth decided to work together and I could talk again.

I stood up with a walker and slowly marched in place. I was quickly exhausted, but I did it. Then I went outside my room for the first time. I had two of my nurses wheel me outside in a wheelchair—outside, in the sun and fresh air. This precious treat away from my bed lasted about ten minutes. The sun wore me out so fast, I needed to get back inside pretty quickly. But…I'd done it.

What the doctors thought would take months had taken days. God, with the help of my doctors, was in charge of my recovery. It's the only explanation.

On August 19, after twenty-five days in the ICU, I was moved to the PCU—the Progressive Care Unit. I was off the ventilator and breathing on my own. Walking with a walker several times a day produced a big appetite.

A day later, on August 20, the cumbersome feeding tube was taken out of my nose and they removed the trach from my neck. The feeding tube had been in place so long, the doctors were worried I might develop an infection in my stomach. With the feeding tube and trach removed, the only thing attached to my body was an oxygen line. I had come so far in such a short amount of time!

The next day, I showered for the first time in three and a half weeks with the help of one of my nurses. Imagine how you might smell after almost four weeks without showering. I probably smelled worse. Just the act of taking a shower took the breath out of me. After we were finished, I went back to my room to nap.

On August 22, I walked up a flight of stairs. Seriously. Granted, I would stop and rest often, but I managed to do it. My mind told my body to get it done, and I did. After every step, my nurses would check my oxygen level to be sure it wasn't dropping too low.

My body felt so slow during physical activities. I had to relearn how to walk. Everything hurt. I've never been so sore in my life.

But the day I climbed the stairs, one of my nurses turned to my mom and said, "He is a true miracle."

From that moment on, I was dubbed "M&M"—The Miracle Man. That is what I came to be known as on the fifth floor at Sharp Grossmont Hospital. To this day, I still get called M&M by professionals in the local medical community. Even my wife's mother, who works at a hospital twenty minutes away, heard about the "Miracle Man".

The nurses couldn't believe my progress. According to them, I was the sickest patient they'd ever seen leave the hospital alive.

five

WITH JESUS

I love sharing the story I just told you in the last chapter. It's a story about overcoming. It's a story about a very broken body becoming whole again. Ultimately, it's a story about God and His ability to perform miracles.

But it's a story that's very rooted in the natural—the physical world we can see. My body, the hospital, the surgeries, the medications, the blood, sweat and tears.

There's more to my story than the physical.

After I woke up from the coma on August 13, I stayed awake for three days. Fear kept me up. If I closed my eyes, would they ever reopen?

One of those nights, I looked at the clock in the ICU. 2:30 a.m. I buzzed the night nurse, Jill. I wasn't able to talk at this point, so I pointed in the direction of the CD player my family had brought into my room. They liked to turn on some light worship music to help me relax and set a peaceful mood in the room. I needed some of that just then.

Jill and the other nurses were really good at understanding what I was trying to say, even though I could only use my hands to communicate and every physical exertion was exhausting. It was like we had a weird language between us, and thank God for that. It was my only way to speak for quite a while.

Jill smiled and moved to the CD player. She pushed play. The CD that happened to be in was my all-time favorite Christian band, Casting Crowns.

For me, this album wasn't just any old record, and I'll tell you why.

I went to Bible college and graduated with my BA in Ministry. My college had a strong focus on missionary work, including short-term overseas missions trips for its students. I had never gone on a missions trip before college, besides going down to Tijuana, which is really common work for churches in San Diego. I loved heading to Mexico and spending time in their local churches, making breakfast for them and playing with the kids.

But I really did want to branch out. I wanted to hop on a plane and go somewhere for a week. So my first year in Bible college, I was stoked when they told us we'd be taking an overseas missions trip. They announced the dates, though not the location, and I told God I was all in...unless we were going to Asia. I just didn't have any desire to visit that continent. No interest. None. I told God that people in London or Maui or the Bahamas needed Jesus. I would go *there*, but not Asia. I simply didn't want to. End of story.

And then they announced our destination: Japan.

To my complete surprise, I was thrilled. Ecstatic, even. God was definitely working in my heart, because suddenly, I wanted nothing more than to share the love of Jesus with the people of Asia. Through my years at Bible college, I ended up traveling to Japan once and China twice. And let me tell you, the beautiful people of Asia are on fire for Jesus. They're incredible. God has now put a passion and love in my heart for Asia.

While in Japan, I heard Casting Crowns for the first time. They had just released their debut album, and it was really speaking to me. In fact, the Holy Spirit spoke to me through that album. In the mornings in Japan, we did personal devotions, and I would read the Word while having this album playing on repeat. Every song had a message, and it was life-changing for me.

When Nurse Jill pressed "play," that particular Casting Crowns album began. The music filled the empty space and took me back to those early mornings in Japan spent close to Jesus and His Word. Jill left the room, and I stared up at the ceiling and simply said in my mind, "Jesus, let's talk."

The next moment, I was in Heaven.

My body stayed on the bed. I didn't die, and I knew it, though I can't explain how. But I was in Heaven—with Jesus. I was sitting on a swing, swinging back and forth. Jesus was on my right on His own swing. The swings were made of beautiful, light-colored wood with knots scattered across the surface. Sort of rustic and natural, but so beautiful. The swings had ropes on either side of them. A hole was drilled into each corner of the wood, and the ropes disappeared into those holes and were tied beneath.

I looked up. The ropes extended up to the heavens among the clouds, set against a clear blue sky. The Casting Crowns album was playing in Heaven, just as it was in my hospital room. I looked down and saw rolling hills with the greenest, richest, most perfectly kept grass I'd ever seen. It made the grass from a baseball stadium on opening day look ugly.

There was a path about four feet wide of pure white cement running through the hills. Smiling children laughed as they rode their bikes on the path through the grass.

I wish I could explain it better or more fully, but it's impossible. It was so beautiful that I couldn't possibly come up with the words to do it justice.

Heaven was so peaceful, so pure, and I was in awe. Not a single blade of brown grass. Nothing out of place. Nothing old, decaying, rotten or worn. Just perfection.

Incredible.

I turned to look at Jesus. He wore a white robe and from what I could tell, He had a beautiful face. I was completely at peace in His presence and basking in His glory.

A moment passed, and the song came on, "What If His People Prayed." It played as if a war cry from Heaven was being broadcast.

I was amazed. Shocked. Confused.

I turned to Jesus again and said, "Why are you doing this to me?"

Jesus looked at me kindly and said, "Because, my son, when you get out of the hospital and you get better, there are some things you need to go back and tell people." Jesus went on to talk about the words in the song. The lyrics speak of Christians picking up their swords and praying. Seeking God's face with humility and turning from our own wicked ways. Imagine what would happen if we all had a consistent, meaningful prayer life. If we made prayer a daily priority.

Jesus then said, "Imagine if every single Christian dusted off his sword and took a stand for Me. This world would be different if people really took a stand for Me, became prayer warriors, and made it a lifestyle."

That really struck me. I'd always assumed my prayer life was pretty strong, but maybe it wasn't. The more I thought about it, the more I realized we limit ourselves. Special events like prayer rallies and "See You at the Pole" are great, but why are they assigned to one day per year? Why can't we have that kind of passion—that kind of commitment—every single day?

As we continued to swing around Heaven, the next song played: "If We Are The Body." Jesus turned to me and said, "You've got to step up as Christians and help out those who are in trouble and in need. You need to be there as the Body of Christ—to help, to love. So many times, you turn your backs. But if you are the Body of Christ, you must do something."

Was I guilty of this? Was I the kind of person who turned my back?

Not intentionally, no. But I realized that our modern society promotes a private lifestyle. Sure, technology "connects" us—or we think it does, but how many people really know their neighbors anymore? How often are we willing to let people into our *real* lives, not the filtered, photoshopped versions we're willing to share on social media? How often are we praying for our communities, our streets, strangers and friends alike?

I thought of the woman at the well. She wouldn't have talked to Jesus if He hadn't approached her first. She would have quietly drawn her water and gone about her business—head down, focused on her task, just like we are most of the time. And yet inside, she was dying. Just like the world. As Jesus did with that woman, we have to reach out. We have to let the lost and the hurting know about the hope inside us.

This doesn't come for free. It costs. Often, it costs our time, sometimes it costs our money, and it may even cost us our pride. Not everyone takes kindly to the Good News, but this charge is *the* Great Commission. It's not optional. If we don't reach out to a dying world, they'll be stuck with no hope, bound for the fires of Hell.

And Jesus came to save the world so that wouldn't happen.

Jesus and I continued swinging over the beautiful, rolling hills for a while, and then the song "Voice of Truth" began to play. Jesus said, "There are so many voices out there, so many gods out there. My voice is the Voice of Truth and it reigns over all. I am the only God to listen to."

I realized in this moment that my body was whole. There were no lines or tubes in me. No holes. No incisions. I was me, but I had a new body. I have no memory of what I was wearing, but it didn't matter. I was whole and well.

Then Jesus said to me, "You need to choose: Are you for Me or against Me? The time is now! No more fooling around. It is time to get right with Me."

Then we went to Hell.

HELL

Contrary to what the world would like you to believe, Hell is real.

Jesus and I were still swinging, but we weren't in Heaven anymore. We were over a deep, dark, circular pit.

A heavy sense of evil nearly choked me. The evil was so thick, I could see it. I could taste it on my tongue. A fence roughly fifteen feet wide stretched around the edge of the pit. Perched on the fence were evil creatures, total freaks of nature. They smelled like sulfur—rotten eggs. Slimy stuff dripped off of them. Some had two heads. Some had more than two arms. I remember seeing one of these creatures with six arms. Chained to the circular fence that lined the pit, they screeched and screamed.

There was nothing good about these disgusting beasts. They were just plain evil. One of them in particular looked like a monkey, but it wasn't a monkey. Monkeys were created by God, and this thing was something altogether different. Something dark and twisted.

As I was surveying our new surroundings, one of the monkey beasts reached out and tried to grab me. Even though I knew he was tied to a fence and couldn't get to me, terror still overtook me. I leaned to my right and grabbed Jesus's swing.

He turned to me. "What are you doing?"

"The evil monkey is trying to grab me," I replied.

"Go back to your swing. He has no authority over you. You are with Me. I have a hold on your life, and I will never let you go. He has no power or control over you."

Peace flooded me again. The enemy had no power over me because my life belonged to Jesus. It was true in that moment as we swung over Hell, but it's also true now.

Jesus didn't linger over Hell. We returned to the perfect green grass of Heaven for a minute. And then the next moment, I was lying in my bed with my eyes wide open.

What had just happened to me? I couldn't believe it. It was a wholly spiritual experience, and yet it felt so real—more real than anything I had experienced in my life.

After being with Jesus, I couldn't go to sleep. I lay awake contemplating my encounter with Jesus until my mom came that morning. With the help of my trach speaking valve, I told her of my experience and she wrote it all down.

I was quiet and contemplative the rest of the day. My ordeal in the hospital had been physical, of course, and keenly emotional. But now it was spiritual, too.

Why had God chosen me for an experience like this? I was an ordinary, twenty-four-year-old youth pastor. I was nobody special. I hadn't done anything significant in my life. I was no better than anyone else (which is still true).

I wept often that day, treasuring my heavenly encounter with Christ. This encounter touched me deeply, and it continues to affect my faith, even now.

That night, I was alone. My family and visitors had left, and I couldn't sleep. As I lay in bed, my gaze wandered up toward my heart monitor. And there, on top of the machine, sat the same hellish monkey creature that had reached for me as Jesus and I swung by. Now he chirped and gnawed, trying to get my attention. As if I could ignore him. He was only about four or five feet from my bed.

The air in the room felt stifling. There was no peace. Fear enveloped me. I closed my eyes, but sleep eluded me. The monkey creature was right above my head, rolling his hands together.

But I remembered what Jesus said: "He has no power over you."

I closed my eyes again, but instead of trying to sleep, I was praying. I called out to Jesus over and over. It's not an exaggeration to say I probably called Jesus's name thousands of times that night. I never slept and finally opened my eyes to watch the horizon shift from inky blue to dusky pink.

The demon monkey was gone.

My mother came early that morning and I told her about what happened. I asked her to call my friend Mark Blum to come to the hospital. Mark is a missionary pastor, and he was the one who had led the trips I took to China. Mark had been to Africa and witnessed incredible demonic activity there. I knew he would believe me, and I hoped he would understand what was happening.

Mark and his wife came to my hospital room right away. They listened to my story, and he laid hands on every part of my ICU room and prayed for God's peace. From the very moment he prayed, my room was filled with the peace of the Lord. I never felt afraid or alone after that.

At the time I got sick, I had been a youth pastor for about four weeks at a church in Ramona. Ramona is the small town just outside San Diego where I grew up. I called my pastor, Pastor Dennis Ottalagano, to come to the hospital so I could tell him about my time with Jesus in Heaven. He sat right across from me. He looked me straight in the eyes, and he listened to every single word I said without interrupting me. I looked like a mess; I was tired and dirty and had an oxygen tube in my nose. As I told him my story, tears ran down my face. "Pastor Dennis," I said, "I need to tell people my story, but they will not believe me."

He encouraged me to tell it anyway. The Lord himself told me to share my story. Who was I to argue? Pastor Dennis said he believed me completely and knew this story needed to be shared. There would be doubters, yes, and we both knew that. I needed to tell my story anyway.

But at that point, I wondered *why*. Why in the world did God ask me to share my story? It was such a personal experience that part of me wondered why it would be of interest to anyone else. It was meaningful for me, but would it be for them?

The Lord was about to answer my *why*.

seven

PRAYERS

August 24, 2009. I had been in the hospital for thirty days, and now it was time to go home. *Home.* Not to a rehab facility, but actually home. I had gotten comfortable inside the walls of the hospital, but I was excited to begin my recovery—to live the rest of my life.

Still, fear clung to me. What if my health tanked again? There would be no nurses or doctors there to help me. What if I went to sleep and didn't wake up? Leaving the hospital and climbing into my parents' car was an exercise in faith.

We took the forty-five-minute drive home to the hills of East San Diego County, where I would recover at my parents' house for the next fourteen months.

I stood before the door of my sister's old bedroom—the room I should have died in—and shook my head. Images of my body lying in that bed, stiff and cold, the way my parents would have found me if I hadn't woken up coughing blood, flashed through my mind. Nope. Couldn't do it. I told my mom there was no way I could bring myself to step foot in there, let alone sleep in that bed. So I would spend the next six months sleeping on a blow-up mattress at the foot of my parents' bed before I felt mentally strong enough to brave the other room.

It might be overstating things to say I "slept" much in those six months. I was horribly uncomfortable. I had to sleep on my back because of the oxygen line going into my nose and because of the large hole in my neck. The incision from the tracheostomy had not healed yet.

My first morning home, I woke up around seven a.m., and I was exhausted. Desperate for a more comfortable position and a little more sleep, I crawled up on my parents' bed and crashed. I don't know how long I slept before I was awakened by my phone vibrating on my parents' dresser. It was my dad calling from work to check on me. As I lifted my arm to answer his call, I was met with a nasty shock. My arm was covered in blood. So was my chest. And the sheets—the whole bed. It was like a horror movie.

I yelled with whatever voice I could muster. "Mom! Come upstairs!"

As I stared at the blood covering everything, my brain finally registered what had happened. I had fallen asleep on my stomach, and blood was oozing out of the hole in my neck. A *lot* of blood.

My mother took one look at me and moved into action. She grabbed me and my oxygen machine and threw us in the car. I was extremely pale and feeling very lightheaded. My mom rushed me to the family doctor, who, thankfully, was only six minutes away. If we'd had to drive far, it might have meant the difference between life and death. My mom called a very good family friend of ours and former nurse, Carolyn Berg, and asked her to meet us at the doctor's office.

We were in such a rush, I showed up to the doctor in just shorts. No shirt or shoes. I didn't have the energy to be embarrassed about this, because suddenly I was having flashbacks to my emergency room check-in.

Our family doctor was immediately concerned about my blood loss. I had already lost so much, and it wasn't slowing down. If he couldn't get the bleeding under control, I would die right there in his office. I was drifting in and out of consciousness, weakening by the second and becoming increasingly confused about what was happening.

In a moment of frustration, the doctor yelled out loud, "We have to get this blood to clot now!"

My mom and Carolyn grabbed hands and began praying out loud to our amazing Father for my neck to clot right away. As soon as they said, "Amen," my doctor became still.

"I can't believe it," he said. "The blood clotted." From that moment, not one drop of blood dripped out of my neck. Praise the name of Jesus!

Though at the time, my praises felt weak and conflicted. I couldn't believe this was happening. After everything I had gone through, now we were dealing with this? Would it ever end?

What should have felt like a triumph—and it absolutely *was* a triumph of the faithful prayers of two God-loving women—left me feeling defeated. I started to cry. I was done. I just wanted to be normal again. But instead, I was frustrated, angry and exhausted.

But let me tell you guys something…I know exactly how I pulled through those dark moments. I know exactly why I'm still here.

Prayer.

"If my people, who are called by my name, will humble themselves and pray and seek my face and turn from their wicked ways, then will I hear from heaven and will forgive their sin and will heal their land."

—2 Chronicles 7:14

The power of prayer is *real*. Without prayer, I know I would not be alive today. I'm wholly convinced that prayer saved me from multiple emergencies and sustained my family and me in those terrible in-between moments of waiting.

If you need proof, let me lay out the prayer timeline of my illness.

I mentioned that the morning I went into the hospital, my mom called Jan. Jan then alerted several of the churches in Ramona to pray. That same morning, my dad called Valerie Balcombe, who was the pastor's wife of their church, and he asked her to start the prayer chain. Within only a couple of hours, thousands upon thousands of people were lifting me up to the Lord Jesus Christ, begging God for His mercy in my crisis.

Prayer requests spread like wildfire all over the world. When I first woke from the coma, I turned on my cell phone and was astonished to discover a text message from someone in Italy whom I didn't even know. How amazing is that? I was on a prayer chain in Italy!

I received another text message from a lady in Connecticut. She wrote that she would probably never meet me in this life, but I was on her prayer chain and she was lifting me up to God for complete healing. As I continued to read all my texts, emails and cards people had sent from all over the world, I was astounded. I didn't know many of these people personally, and yet they were fervently praying for me day after day. I pulled through crisis after crisis while these friends and strangers cried out to God on my behalf.

Wow!

This is the body of Christ. The outpouring of prayer touched me deeply and in a way I'll never forget, but it made me think about something else—the impact technology could have on the church.

We already recognize that technology has forever changed our world, but have you ever thought about how our electronically connected society has positively impacted prayer? The thousands and thousands of people across the world who prayed for me would never have heard that I needed prayer without the Internet. By the time news of our urgent need reached anyone by snail mail, I probably would have been dead.

Can you imagine if the church used the Internet to pray for others on a continual basis? Can you imagine how the world would change? It's so ironic. The Internet is a cesspool of pornography and many other disgusting examples of violence and nonsense, but God causes all things to work for the good of those who are called according to His purpose. God can redeem *anything,* and that's certainly true of the Internet. We can use our wonderfully connected world to spread good, joyous, God-honoring things, too.

The next time you open up your email or hop on your phone to send someone a text, shoot a friend or family member a message telling them you love them or are thinking about them. Shoot them a quick encouraging note that will brighten their day, or let them know they popped up in your mind and you are praying for them. Little notes like these go a very long way, and they only take a few seconds. That's one easy, excellent way to use the Internet for good.

Recently, I spoke at my home church and gave my testimony. When the topic of prayer came up, I mentioned something that the Lord has really been working on in my life. So many times, I am on my social media sites, or even in my inbox, and I see a lot of requests for prayer. How often do we keep scrolling? How often do we skip over these requests? Even with the powerful demonstration of prayer's impact in my life, I have been tempted to bypass these messages from time to time.

But God really pressed it on my heart to *always* pray when someone asks. I am so thankful that thousands of people decided to take a minute and pray for my situation. I would not be here today if they decided to keep scrolling.

I told my church family that we must stop to pray when we come across social media posts asking for prayer. I have committed myself to doing this, and it has been such a blessing to lift up my brothers and sisters in need. Isn't that the way it works with God? The things He asks us to do end up blessing us! I encourage you to practice this discipline. You might be surprised at how much you find yourself uplifted.

God is so rad. Check this out: Remember those missions trips to Japan and China I told you about? Well, when I was in my coma on life support, my friends in China were hosting a week-long prayer meeting. One of my stateside friends emailed my photo to one of the missionaries in China. She told them what was going on with me and how I needed immediate prayer. The missionary printed out photos of my face on little cards and handed them out to all the attendees. They said, "When we pray, this is the guy we are praying for." The missionary also put my photo on a very large video screen and, as a group, they prayed for me at the meeting. And suddenly, hundreds of people in China were praying for me.

None of the steps that led up to this were coincidences. This is God! He drew me to a place I thought I never wanted to visit. He formed bonds between me and my brothers and sisters there. And in my time of crisis, those brothers and sisters in China sent up thousands of prayers on my behalf.

Not a coincidence.

Powerful prayers during my time of illness had an impact on the hospital where I was staying, too. Because of prayer warriors lifting me up around the world, I got a whole new identity in the hospital. To the doctors and nurses, I was no longer Jonathan Rizzo. I was their Miracle Man. The day of my release, they lined the hallways to cheer for me. They took photos as I walked down the hall with my cane, my mom carrying my oxygen tank behind me.

I can't recall exact details—which doctors and nurses were there—but it felt like everyone who had ever cared for me was in those hallways. Maybe even Dr. Fox and Nurse Laila, the doctor and nurse from my first day in the E.R., were there. They ended up getting married years later!

I'm not sure who was more emotional—me or those medical professionals who had poured so much into my care.

That was some walk down the hall. I was forty-two pounds lighter than I had been a month before. My shorts were nearly falling off of me.

As I passed by, one of the nurses pulled me aside. With a tear in his eye, he whispered to me, "We didn't know what was wrong with you. We ran over a hundred tests. We ran tests on you that people have never heard of to try to figure out what was wrong. You were a guinea pig to us. We had to run tests we had never done before. But before we did any of this, all of the nurses gathered together in a circle, held hands, and prayed to the Lord Jesus for His wisdom and guidance."

Tears poured down my face. I looked at him, and all I could say was, "Thank you."

I know for certain I wouldn't be here today if it weren't for brothers and sisters answering the call for urgent prayer. I wouldn't be here if the church of Christ hadn't cried out to God for my life.

Too often, we fall asleep and neglect the call to pray. That has to stop now. We have to remember the power prayer can have in our lives and the lives of others. I hope that every person reading this book will be inspired to pray more.

"After he had dismissed them, he went up on a mountainside by himself to pray. When evening came, he was there alone."

—Matthew 14:23

This is one of my favorite verses in Scripture. Christ's life was steeped in prayer. That's what we're supposed to shoot for, too! I pray that I can imitate Christ in the prayer life He practiced.

Sometimes when we pray, we expect Him to instantly move according to our timetable. There were many people who laid hands on me when I was sick, but I wasn't instantly healed. Nine years later, I'm still not completely healed. But I'm alive, and I'm improving daily.

Sometimes after we pray, we make the mistake of speaking words of doubt and disbelief over the prayers we've just spoken. This undermines our prayers. Sometimes it's tough to believe in the power of our prayers because there have been times we haven't seen God move on our behalf. Always remember, God is God. He moves on His timetable, and He absolutely knows what is best for us at every moment. He is not our robot doing everything we tell Him, the moment we tell Him to. God is the Creator of the Universe. He can do it all in His perfect timing.

"I will exalt you, my God the King, I will praise your name for ever and ever. Every day I will praise you and extol your name for ever and ever."

—Psalm 145:1–2

Do we believe God has the power to answer our prayers? Do we believe He hears us when we pray? I do. If I didn't get it before, believe me, I get it now. Please don't miss this point. Prayers are just words if they are not spoken in faith to the Lord. Prayer is powerful because of *Whom* we're praying to.

I have learned firsthand the impact prayer can have on a person's life. I have seen with my own eyes the dynamic nature of the words we speak to God. It was a lesson I needed, since I had been speaking death into my future for many years.

WORDS

"The tongue has the power of life and death,
and those who love it will eat its fruit."

—*Proverbs 18:21*

I always had a feeling I would die before I turned twenty-five. Something inside me told me I wouldn't see my twenty-fifth birthday. And I said so. Often.

I don't know where this feeling came from. I don't know why this deep sense had invaded my being, but I know it wasn't from the Lord.

The girl I was dating when I got sick heard this from me all the time. "I won't make it to twenty-five, anyway." Or, "Well, I'm going to die young." She would rebuke me every time.

And then, fifty-two days before my twenty-fifth birthday, I was in a coma. Fifty-two days before I turned twenty-five, I wasn't expected to make it through the night. Before I got sick, I hadn't understood what my girlfriend meant when she would say, "Words have power. Take it back. You're not going to die young."

After I got sick, I understood I'd been speaking death into my life. I'd been proclaiming doom over my future and giving Satan authority over me that he wouldn't otherwise have. Words have power, and I hadn't been respecting the power of my words.

Remember when I told you I would eventually understand the *why* of God saving me? It has to do with words.

God allowed what He did in my life because I needed to share this story—share it with you through this book, one-on-one when I talk to people I meet and when speaking to groups around the country. The words of this story are full of powerful truths about who God is and what He has done in the life of one ordinary person.

I was on prayer chains at a lot of different churches when I was sick. Because of that, I was invited to speak at several of those churches in the months following my release from the hospital. I spoke at Living Way Church—the church my family attended. I had attended from the time I was first in youth group in sixth grade.

Living Way Church holds a very special place in my heart, so I was thrilled when I was invited to share my testimony one Sunday morning. After I had spoken, an elderly lady approached me, pushing her daughter in a wheelchair. Her daughter was in an accident many years before, and she had experienced significant head trauma.

The mother, having heard my testimony minutes earlier, asked me to repeat what Heaven was like. As I was explaining this to her, tears began to roll down her face.

When I was finished, she told me that when her daughter was in her accident, she was in a coma. When she woke from her coma, she told her mom that she was in Heaven, playing with Jesus on hills of beautiful green grass. Just like what I had experienced.

Now the tears started running down my cheeks. I thanked her for sharing this with me, and then I thanked the Lord for confirming the reality of the experience to *both* of us. My testimony was powerful for this mother, but her story was equally powerful for me.

Not long after I spoke at Living Way, I spoke about my experience to the youth group kids at my home church one evening. There were about thirty kids there, and they had been heavily affected by my illness. I was their youth pastor, after all. They were afraid I might die.

After youth group ended, one of my students came up to me and told me I had to talk to her mom when she came for pick-up. When her mom arrived, she told me a story.

My student, her mom, and her dad lived in the Middle East before coming to the United States. One day, back when they lived overseas, they were driving and got into a very bad car accident. Her father died instantly. My student was okay, but her mom was in a coma for three months.

She said while she was in her coma, she was swinging in Heaven with Jesus. She went into great detail about how beautiful and green the grass was. She swung in Heaven over green grass.

I started to cry, and then I just grabbed her and hugged her. God is so good! Somehow, the two of us had ended up on the same side of the world to share our stories with each other.

Those were some powerful words for both of us.

When my wife, Lindsay, and I got married, we were praying for a church to attend. We chose a beautiful church in North San Diego County, and that became our new place of fellowship. We got really involved in this church family and met some amazing lifelong friends.

We met one young couple there, and they were the greatest people. She had a sister who lived in Texas, and this sister had a few kids. One day, we got a call on the prayer chain that one of her children, who was about two years old, had a bad case of pneumonia. It was so bad, he was in the hospital. We all prayed for this little boy. A few days later, things took a turn for the worse and that little one left this earth and entered Heaven.

Sometime later, the pastor of our church asked me to tell my story during the service one Sunday morning. Everything about this day was powerful. I remember it so clearly. The presence of the Lord was so strong in that building this particular morning. After I spoke, our friend pulled me to the back of the church and asked to speak to me.

In tears, she told me that when her nephew passed away, she got a call from her dad, telling her the news that this precious little boy had gone to be with Jesus. Her father said that when he found out, God gave him a specific vision. The vision was of his grandson and Jesus playing together and running on the most beautiful green, grassy hills he'd ever seen. His grandson was smiling.

God uses words. God uses stories. We all have different gifts that God uses to help build His kingdom. I keep telling you I'm just an ordinary guy and there was no particular reason for God to save me when He did. But, just like you, I do have some gifts. Some of my gifts are hospitality, generosity and encouragement. I like people, and I know a lot of them. God equipped me to speak and share in front of large groups. Because of this particular grouping of gifts, my story has traveled pretty far. These powerful words that are all about God's power have touched people's hearts and increased their faith. And the words shared back with me have been just as impactful. They have built my faith and touched my heart.

Words have power and value in the spiritual realm.

As we walk in this life, our words have great value in the spiritual kingdom. Everything begins in the spiritual realm. Power is released in the spiritual realm and manifests in the natural. That's why prophetic words are so important. They release power when the Holy Spirit leads the person giving them.

"Out of the same mouth come praise and cursing.
My brothers, this should not be."

—*James 3:10*

Even our regular, everyday words have power. The Bible says we will be held accountable for every word that comes out of our mouths. I don't think many of us understand how significant that is. If we did, coarse joking in casual conversations would disappear from our vocabulary. We wouldn't let words like, "You're stupid. I hate you. You're ugly. You suck," escape our lips.

Instead, we should look to uplift people. We should be dropping word blessings. Since I've been writing this book, I've been doing an experiment. I've listened to conversations of both Christians and non-Christians. Sometimes I can't tell the difference in their words. The Christians might not be swearing or using vulgar language, but they are cursing each other when they spew negativity and judgment and unkindness. Power is going out, and the devil is rubbing his hands together, enjoying the empowerment we are giving him. He can't operate if we are praising the Lord and our fellow man with our tongues.

Praise from our mouth is a weapon of warfare that we need to utilize for our fellow brothers and sisters. When Paul was in prison, he and Silas began singing praises at midnight and the chains that bound them fell to the ground. Our praise is the most precious thing that we can offer God if our heart is completely centered on Him.

I often think back to when I was lying in my hospital bed between life and death, listening to music. The music and powerful lyrics of those songs sustained me and lifted my spirits.

I challenge you, as I challenge myself, to bless people with your words. If you determine to do that and do it often, pretty soon it will become a habit. Once we release a word, we are never able to bring it back, so imagine if those words were words of life and love.

Jesus knew the power of His words. He spoke, and Lazarus rose. He spoke, and the centurion's servant was healed.

Jesus gave His followers a weapon to use, but our weapons are not of steel. Our weapon in this battle against the forces of evil is our tongue. The question we have to ask ourselves is, are we using our weapon against the enemy, or against God's people? The choice is ours, and too often, the church is eating itself alive instead of wielding this powerful weapon against our true enemy.

Jesus gave us the keys to the kingdom, and the main key that unlocks all this power is our tongue. That's why Satan used it against me when I declared out loud I would not live to be twenty-five years old.

"When we put bits into the mouths of horses to make them obey us, we can turn the whole animal. Or take ships as an example. Although they are so large and driven by strong winds, they are steered by a very small rudder wherever the pilot wants to go. Likewise the tongue is a small part of the body, but it makes great boasts. Consider what a great forest is set on fire by a small spark. The tongue also is a fire, a world of evil among the parts of the body. It corrupts the whole person, sets the whole course of his life on fire, and is itself set on fire by hell."

—James 3:3–6

Words have the power of life and death. Does that sound dramatic? It is, but it doesn't make it less true. Human existence plays out in the dramas of life and death. God's glory is revealed in the dramas of life and death, and my time in the hospital is only one example of many billions. I'd like to tell you about two more.

nine

LIFE & DEATH:
A TRIBUTE TO RYAN AND RORY

I absolutely love baseball. I could go on and on about my love for this sport, but that's not what this book is about. But trust me, I *could* write a whole book about how much I love baseball.

When I was on disability for those fourteen months, I wanted to get away. I needed to recover, to rediscover *life*. I wanted to remember "normal," and baseball has always been a part of my "normal."

So I went to Phoenix for the Padres' spring training that year. One of my best friends, Titus, his wife and two beautiful daughters live in Phoenix. I stayed on their couch for about two months and went to spring training every day.

I woke up on one of those clear, bright March mornings and started my day so I could get to the fields right when the players started to come out. I plugged in my phone to charge and hopped in the shower. When I got out, I grabbed my phone and saw that I had a missed call from Pastor Dennis and several from my dad.

I dialed my dad back in a hurry. He answered, but his normally strong, loud voice sounded…different; quiet, broken, and shaken. He delivered news to me that no one wants to hear. My best friend of thirteen years,

Ryan Cupples, had been killed in a car accident a few hours earlier.

I couldn't believe it. I refused to believe it.

I don't remember exactly what I said. I asked a few questions, I think, and hung up the phone. I sat on the couch for a while, staring into space. It was impossible to process, and I honestly felt like it was some sort of bad dream that I would wake up from.

It wasn't.

This was actually happening; Ryan had passed away at the age of twenty-four. My brain didn't seem able to process it. I was just…numb.

I got up off the couch and drove to Peoria to see the Padres' batting practice. I went about my day normally, as if I hadn't gotten some of the most terrible news of my life. But then it began to hit me. I would never see Ryan again. I would never hear his voice again. I would never play one-on-one basketball with him. I would never go to the beach with him again.

Ryan was more than a friend; he was my brother. My family and his family were very close. My sister and his sister are lifelong best friends. And I was never going to see him again.

The days leading up to his memorial service were rough. I was extremely emotional. I cried a lot. I experienced sadness, anger and confusion. All the memories from growing up with him played through my head like a movie on a loop. Ryan and I did everything together. He had his entire life in front of him. He was young and healthy. He was working in the field he'd always wanted to get into. This was all taken from him in a second. And *he* was taken from *us*.

Ryan's dad, Mick, is a pastor. Mick is an amazing man of God and a great husband and father. Mick did the memorial service for his son. To this day, I don't know how he kept himself together throughout the service. God carried him through it, that's for sure. What a beautiful service. More than five hundred people filled the church. It was so crowded that they had to have an extra room for overflow, and that was standing room only. Not only did the memorial service honor Ryan, more importantly, it honored God. You could feel the presence of the Lord in that church.

I was fortunate enough to be one of the four people who spoke at the service. I shared some very funny stories about Ryan and me. He was an incredible friend to me.

But I didn't only share lighthearted stories. With the microphone in my hand, I said, "This should be me, not Ryan. Eight months ago, I was in the hospital fighting for my life. There's no way I should be up here talking right now. I don't understand why God would choose to keep me here but take Ryan, but I do know that this was His plan. We may not see it right now, but we have to trust the Lord, because His ways are so much better than our ways."

I gave Mick a big hug, then went and sat back down, my face wet with tears.

Mick didn't just honor his son during the service. He laid out the Gospel message of Jesus, no holds barred. It was like we were in church.

Here is the coolest part about it: There were so many people there who may have never stepped foot into church, but they were there because Ryan was a very popular and well-liked young man. More than five hundred people heard the Gospel that day. I don't know if they gave their lives to Jesus that evening or not, but what I do know is that because of Ryan, seeds were planted in the hearts of those who otherwise may not have heard how much Jesus loves them. How awesome is that! Ryan made a huge impact on everyone who knew him, and this was true even after his life on earth was complete.

When our second daughter was born, my wife and I hadn't settled on a name for her. The day before we left the hospital to go home, we had been in continual prayer that God would give us a name we would agree on, and that it would fit our new little blessing from God.

My wife, Lindsay, knew how close Ryan and I were. She asked me, "Wouldn't it be awesome to honor Ryan and name the baby Evelyn Ryanne?"

I'm not going to lie. I cried like a broken fire hydrant. And so we named our girl Evelyn Ryanne. Ryan's name lives on, and so does his memory. He will never be forgotten by those who loved him. I still miss him every day.

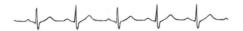

I had a very good friend named Rory who worked at a Christian retail shop that sold clothes and Christian CDs at a mall in San Diego. When I was about twenty years old, I walked into that store, and with a big smile on his face, he approached me, introduced himself, and asked if there was anything for which I needed prayer. I told him what I was going through at that time, and he asked if he could pray for me right then and there. He put his arm around me and prayed the most powerful prayer.

At this time, I was a drummer in a rock band, and Rory would come to many of our shows. He would also promote our music at shows and in the store where he worked. He left such an impression on me that we exchanged contact information and became very close. Although he was a year younger, I looked up to him as a genuine man of God. Randomly, he would call or text during the day to check up on me and keep me accountable in my walk with God. Naturally, he would be praying for me.

Rory answered the call of God on his life and volunteered as one of the youth leaders in a church in North San Diego County. He started some Bible studies in this part of town, as well. When I was in the coma, Rory was volunteering with a group of about twenty or thirty teenagers. They went on a weeklong summer camp trip up north. Not long after they arrived at their destination, Rory and several of the kids were playfully jumping off rocks into a lake and swimming. Rory jumped, and then he never returned to the surface. About an hour later, they found his body roughly thirty feet below.

I was told of Rory's death the day after I got out of the hospital. Guilt washed over me. Rory was a better person than I was. I looked up to him. I was angry, and I questioned God over and over. Why him and not me? Why? I thought of Rory as more spiritual than I was. He had done a lot more for Christ and the Kingdom than I had. So why did God allow a great person like Rory to die and not me? I didn't know. I still don't know. All I do know is that He causes all things to work for the good of those who are called according to His purpose.

Someone I know went to Rory's funeral in San Diego, and he said that about two thousand people were there. At his service, several people surrendered their lives to Christ because of the testimony of Rory's life. I can sit here writing this today knowing that if just one person would come to know Jesus because of it, Rory would have gladly given his life for them. He was the embodiment of laying down his life for others, and this was true even in his death.

We can't predict the day of our death, nor is there a formula in life to help us ensure we will escape bad outcomes. The only thing we can be sure of is that someday we will die, and if Jesus is our Lord and Savior, we will spend eternity with Him. If not, we will spend eternity in the fires of Hell without relief.

Is God still faithful even in times of death? Absolutely! God uses everything for His Kingdom so that all may know His Son. The people who received Christ at Rory's funeral will tell their friends, and those people will tell their friends. It's like throwing a rock into a pond and watching the ripples spread. That's how Rory's and Ryan's lives and deaths were used for the Kingdom of God.

Listen, friends. No one knows when their time is up. Life can end in a moment. Jesus could return in a moment. I'm not really the type of person who goes onto the street corner and yells at people, scaring them with pronouncements of fire and brimstone. I don't really believe that's effective.

But I am the kind of person who will say things I know to be true. And this is true: We all will die. And when we do, we will either spend eternity with Jesus in paradise, or we will spend eternity separated from Him in Hell. Heaven is real, and so is Hell. I've seen them both.

"For to me, to live is Christ and to die is gain."

—Philippians 1:21

ten

GET SERIOUS WITH JESUS

Early in the morning on July 26, 2009, Dr. Fox told me I wouldn't remember the next few days—if I survived them at all.

I crossed my arms over my chest and lay back. I said my prayer and before I was put into a coma, peace descended on me. Whenever I try to describe this peace, words fail me. I can't do it justice. It was rich and deep—a peace from God. I know it wasn't something from me because before I got sick, I had been afraid to die. But now that I faced the real possibility of it, God gave me serenity beyond imagining.

In this peace, I simply *knew* God was with me, whether I woke up from this coma or not.

Nothing—no person, no amount of money, no pleasure, no other god—can give you peace like our Lord and Savior Jesus Christ, a peace that surpasses all understanding. Maybe you've heard something like that from the Bible, in Philippians. I had heard it hundreds of times. But today, this isn't a mere maxim to me. It's not just a Christian saying. This is truth. I have experienced it firsthand.

I was gasping for each breath. Every indication the doctors gave said I wouldn't live, yet I was still at peace. Surrounded by His peace. I wasn't going into a panic. I was completely at rest throughout my entire body. I did not understand why at such a time of crisis, but I knew it was from the Lord. Facing a prognosis that gave me three hours to live, only He could put my mind and soul at ease.

Where does this peace of the Lord come from? It comes from knowing beyond all doubt that God is real and that we are reconciled to Him through His Son, Jesus Christ. Simple—and deep and wide and mind-blowing—as that.

> *"To the angel of the church in Laodicea write: These are the words of the Amen, the faithful and true witness, the ruler of God's creation. I know your deeds, that you are neither cold nor hot. I wish you were either one or the other! So, because you are luke-warm—neither hot nor cold—I am about to spit you out of my mouth."*
>
> *—Revelation 3:14–16*

This is the last message to the last church in Revelation. It's really important that we realize this message is for us, now! We are the Laodicean Church. In the Western church, there is complacency. It's lukewarm. God wants us hot. He wants all of us. Not fifty percent, not ninety percent, but one hundred percent. Too many lukewarm messages have arisen to placate everyone's desires, disregarding the true message of Jesus Christ. Perhaps, that's the reason Jesus answered my call when I said, "Jesus, let's talk."

When I was on the swing in Heaven, Jesus was alluding to the fact that we must choose. There is no gray area. We are either going to serve the Lord all the way, or not at all. And while we may feel like we have all the time in the world to draw that line and take our stand, we have no idea how many minutes are left to us. I think of Ryan, Rory, and myself—we were all halfway into our twenties when death came knocking. We never know the number of our days, and so we must choose. Now.

Friends, the time is now to get right with the Lord. There really is no more fooling around. Take a stand! Are you with Christ or against Him? In the book of Revelation, we read Jesus's warning to John, written thousands of years ago, and He is warning us too: If you are neither hot nor cold, He will spit you out of His mouth.

That sounds harsh, but those are the words Jesus Himself used when He spoke to John.

Jesus told me that this is what He wanted me to bring back to His people when I got out of the hospital. In my opinion, Christ will be back sooner than some might think. Again, take a look at Genesis before the flood. People were doing what they wanted. The only intent in their hearts was evil. I hate to tell you this, but you're probably well aware already that there is a lot of evil in our world today. How long will Christ delay in His return? We cannot know, and so we need to own our faith in Christ today.

Pastor Dennis, my pastor when I was working at the church in Ramona, would say every Sunday, "There is a hitching post outside. Before you come in, leave your religion there. Come inside, and let's talk about having a personal relationship with Jesus Christ."

Being "religious" is not going to get us to Heaven. I don't really like the word "religion," personally. Anyone can be religious. A religious person can go to church, put a few bucks in the plate, know the Scriptures, and not have a personal relationship with Jesus. Look at the Pharisees, the religious leaders in Jesus's day. Religion was their lifestyle, but they lacked the relationship part with the Lord. The Pharisees were the group most heavily criticized by Jesus. They had religion and no relationship with Him.

So often, we get caught up in this world. What will people give up for material gains in this world? Look around you. Some people have given up eternity for money, a bigger house, a better car, a life of pleasure, or fame. They will spend their lives pursuing these earthly, material possessions. As a Christian, our pursuit should be eternity. Not just for us, but for the people all around us.

Words. Those powerful, life-saving words of the Gospel are why I'm still alive. And they should be at the center of our lives as Christians.

When was the last time you told someone about Jesus? When was the last time you invited a friend to church? When was the last time you prayed for the sick? These things should be in our hearts. I can't tell you how often I fall down on the job here. How often do we get complacent? But we can make a recommitment to God right here, right now. Are you ready to get serious with God?

It wasn't a religious experience that I had when the peace of God came over me in the emergency room. I was experiencing a heightened relationship with Jesus Christ. I knew that if God decided to take me home at twenty-four years old, I would be going to Heaven. I knew that deep in my soul. Though the doctors were scurrying around and the nurses were sticking needles and tubes in my arms, I had a deep feeling of contentment.

You see, my friends, this is why we live. We live for the day we will be with Jesus for eternity. Please don't miss that. I hope this testimony gives you great hope. That day is going to be the greatest day of your life. I can say that with confidence because I was on the border between two worlds, experiencing what each would feel like. Let me tell you, the beginning of eternity with Jesus is a day worth living for. It's a day worth dedicating your whole life to Christ for.

Each day I live, until I enter paradise again, my goal is to bring glory to God in every single thing I say, think and do. What about you? Are you eternally minded? Friends, I don't ask you this because I'm judging you. I say this to challenge you, the same as I challenge myself. I say this to remind you that our lives are merely vapor. We are here today, and before you know it, our time will be up.

Don't waste your life in the pursuit of things. Your time here on earth is very precious. You only get one chance to fulfill the purpose for which you were created.

If I didn't have a relationship with Jesus that very scary morning, I know I wouldn't have been content with dying. Terror, not peace, would have seized me. Fear, not acceptance, would have overtaken me. What about you?

I'm not saying my illness was filled with *only* peace and assurance. It was a roller coaster of emotions. I've told you about that—the anger, weariness, frustration, heartache. But in that moment—in the life-or-death moment where I stared at the real possibility of death and prayed to my God—I had peace. And that is solely because of my relationship with the Lord.

You may be asking yourself, "Can I really have a relationship with God after all the terrible things I've done, the garbage I've brought into my life?"

Yes! You can. Jesus went to the cross and shed His blood for everyone! He took on the sins of every single person, no matter what we've done! That includes *you*.

It's never too late to get right with the Lord. Whether you accept the Lord at age five, or seventy-five, you're never too old or too young to experience the love of God. If you're sitting in jail convicted of murder, it's never too late to accept Jesus. The apostle Paul was a murderer. King David had Bathsheba's husband killed. And yet these men were loved and used by God. He redeemed them from themselves. God's grace and forgiveness know no bounds.

I think about Jesus when He was on the cross. He had one criminal on either side of Him. One of them, with his life ebbing away, asked Jesus to remember him in paradise. Jesus didn't look at him and say, "No, you're a thief. I can't take you with me to eternity." Jesus is the God of second, third, fourth, fifth, infinity chances. He is always ready to receive us into His family.

If you ask Him, He will come into your life right now. Just pray:

"Lord Jesus, I ask you to be my Savior right now. I invite you into my life and into my heart. I know I am a sinner, and I know you died on the cross for my sins. I want to live a life that is pleasing to you. Amen."

If you said that simple prayer, and meant it, He will come into your life. He will complete you. You will never be alone again and when you die, you will be with Him in eternity. The choice is yours. Please don't miss it.

Several people have asked me this question: "How is your life different now that you have been given a second chance? What have you learned from this encounter with Jesus?"

If you knew me before my hospital stay, you would know I am just as crazy now as I was before. I'm still the same guy. I'm still the loud, funny guy who likes to play hard and experience everything life has to offer.

But my perspective has changed. I realize how short life is. How fragile we are. We don't have to be terrified by that truth. But we should let that truth be real to us. If that truth is real to us, we won't put off matters of eternal significance. If that truth is real to us, we won't wait until tomorrow to secure our souls.

eleven

WHAT, NOT WHY

This probably doesn't come as news to you, but life flat-out sucks sometimes. I could lie and tell you that because I saw Jesus face-to-face in Heaven, everything is sunshine and roses all the time. But it's not.

Even though I had seen Jesus face-to-face in Heaven, lying in that hospital bed, I was angry with Him sometimes. I was in the ICU bed with tubes running throughout my body, living off liquids going through my nose.

Why didn't God just take me home? Why couldn't I have stayed in Heaven?

I had heard everything the doctors had told me about my recovery. Rehab for months. I may never walk again. A good chance I'd never work again. I would have to relearn everything—talking, writing, spelling. I would have to relearn to use my arms and legs, to sit up, to sit down. It sounded like too much to handle.

And I looked terrible. For a while, I refused to look in the mirror. My eyeballs bulged from the medication; my face was gaunt and completely sunken in from losing so much weight. I looked like a sack of bones. At that moment, dying seemed a lot easier than dealing with this uphill battle I was facing. And what would be at the end of the uphill battle? We had no idea. Maybe I would fight and fight and still never have a normal, healthy life again.

At times, I begged God to allow me to die. I hate to admit that now, but it's the truth.

Bruce, a good friend of my family, talked to my dad while I was in the hospital. He said, "The question we need to ask ourselves is not *why* are we in this situation, but rather *what* good will come from it." When my dad encouraged me with this, it instantly changed my perspective on the situation.

I don't know about you, but I can complain about stuff. A lot. When things are rough, it's easy to ask questions. Why me? Why this again, God? What did I do to deserve this? These questions are natural, but they're not helpful. We don't often get to know why. We don't get access to God's big picture right away, and sometimes we may never know why certain things happen in our lives. This is a much more helpful question: What good can come from this situation? God brings positive things—God brings good— even from the roughest patches of our lives.

When I was able to shift my perspective to ask the *what*, it was so much easier to understand the *why*. I had to share my story because there were people who needed to hear it. What good was going to come of my illness? Changed lives. Helping build the Kingdom of God. Deepened faith for me and for others. Those are some big *whats*. Those *whats* matter, and the more I thought about them, the less I asked things like, "Why me?"

> *"For I know the plans I have for you," declares the Lord,*
> *"plans to prosper you and not to harm you, plans to give you*
> *hope and a future."*
>
> *—Jeremiah 29:11*

We often hear things like "God has a plan for you." In fact, we hear it so often, it's become a cliché. Maybe we even tune it out, especially when we're going through hard times. But it's true. When bad stuff has happened, it doesn't mean God has forgotten us. He brings good out of even the worst situations. He had a plan for me in my illness. And He has a plan for every single person reading this book, no matter what you're going through.

One night during my hospital stay, my brother-in-law, Gabe, was stuck in my ICU room during shift change. He wasn't allowed to leave in the middle of a shift change, so he was basically trapped in there for two hours with me. I remember sitting up as straight as possible in my flimsy hospital gown at this little table in my room. It was very close to my bed, as my tubes kept me tethered to the machines beside my bed.

He sat across the small table from me. Just sitting there was a challenge for me. My body was so weak, it didn't want to stay upright and I barely had the muscle control to force it. But sitting at that table was such a welcome change from lying in bed all day long.

Gabe started out by praying with me. What he went on to share that night was life changing, and I'll never forget it. He shared a passage out of Hebrews 12. The chapter before this, Hebrews 11, is very well known as "the faith chapter." It is an amazing passage of Scripture, but tucked away right after that is Hebrews 12. Hebrews 12:4-13 reads:

> *"In your struggle against sin, you have not yet resisted to the point of shedding your blood. And you have forgotten that word of encouragement that addresses you as sons:*
>
> *'My son, do not make light of the Lord's discipline, and do not lose heart when he rebukes you, because the Lord disciplines those he loves, and he punishes everyone he accepts as a son.' Endure hardship as discipline; God is treating you as sons. For what son is not disciplined by his father? If you are not disciplined (and everyone undergoes discipline), then you are illegitimate children and not true sons. Moreover, we have all had human fathers who disciplined us and we respected them for it. How much more should we submit to*

the Father of our spirits and live! Our fathers disciplined us for a little while as they thought best; but God disciplines us for our good, that we may share in his holiness. No discipline seems pleasant at the time, but painful. Later on, however, it produces a harvest of righteousness and peace for those who have been trained by it. Therefore, strengthen your feeble arms and weak knees. 'Make level paths for your feet,' so that the lame may not be disabled, but rather healed."

Like clay on a potter's wheel, God is shaping us. We're being molded into His image. In this life, we don't start off as a finished product. And the clay has to be heated up before it can become a completed masterpiece. God's children will go through the fires of discipline for His purpose. When you're in the fire, don't ask why. Look to Jesus and ask, "What is the purpose of this storm? What good will come from this heat?"

We can do nothing by ourselves, so it makes sense that He needs to shape us into His image, to carry His glory. He is shaping us through the fire, through trials, to carry His presence, to carry His glory so that the world may come to know Him through our testimony of what He's done through us.

So many times, when we are going through the trials, we want out. When I was in the hospital with nineteen lines and tubes going in and out of my body, I wanted to be out of the hospital. Immediately. Right then. I didn't want to endure another second. I couldn't see it at the time, but God was shaping me physically, emotionally and spiritually through that experience. Often, it takes time for the potter to shape the clay. Every moment I endured was necessary. Every moment contributed to God making me the man He wanted me to be when I walked out of the hospital.

When we pray, we often try to make it on our terms and our timelines. Look at the past five or ten years of your life. Look at how God has delivered you through many trials. We forget to look back at what we have prayed for and what God did in that time, yet that is the strength of our faith to endure whatever we're dealing with right now.

Trials can be difficult to endure, but we have choices in the midst of our trials. We have choices about where we'll put our focus and how we'll face those trials. How are you going to wake up tomorrow? Are you going to focus on Jesus, or are you going to focus on the problems you're facing? It's your choice. Believe me, in the hospital, I wanted to focus on my problems. Jesus practically forced me to focus on Him, and it changed my perspective forever.

My favorite verse of all time is from the book of Proverbs. It is so simple, but it really means a lot to me.

> *"A happy heart makes the face cheerful,*
> *but heartache crushes the spirit."*
>
> *—Proverbs 15:13*

Adversity tries to nudge us away from embracing this verse. Trials tempt us to be negative, sad, pouty, or miserable. But we have a choice; we can wake up each day and give everything to the Lord. We can smile, bless others, and find joy. Will we always feel happy? No, probably not. But happiness and joy are not the same thing. We can always find our joy in the Lord even in the times when we grieve or feel sad.

We serve a *big* God. Trials can be big—they can be huge, even—but they will never be bigger than God. Trials will stretch you, but you will never break. Give your situation to God. The same God who raised people from the dead, who parted the sea, who healed the sick and blind, who performed miracle after miracle after miracle, is the God who is walking with you right now through whatever storm or situation you are facing. Do not give up. Ever. This is part of your story, and the rest is yet to be written.

twelve

EXPENSIVE FAITH

In total, my hospital bill was around 1.1 million dollars. I had insurance, but it didn't cover everything. I was going to specialists three times a week for months. Co-pays add up.

I couldn't work, so I was on disability. Every check that came in went right back out, and then some. I was frustrated and worried. I had to cover my medical bills, and they were piling up at a record rate. But I also had to worry about my car payment, my phone bill and the rest of my everyday living expenses. The world doesn't stop just because you are sick.

I was terrified. I wasn't fully trusting God. The numbers didn't lie. More money was going out than coming in—simple as that. Instead of giving that situation to the Lord, I focused on it myself. From the moment I woke up, to the moment I went to bed, I was worried sick.

I finally realized that if I kept trying to rely on myself to resolve this situation, the numbers would never add up. It was too big a problem, and I was too small a person, so I gave the situation fully to the Lord. I'm still not sure how He made it happen, but I paid off all my bills. It was all God!

Sometimes things appear hopeless. In those moments especially, having faith in God takes immense courage. When we embrace faith, we don't look at the here and now—the big, scary problem we're facing—but we choose to defy natural law and look at those things that are waiting for us in the spiritual realm.

I can be sure that one of three things is true about every person reading this book: one, you are currently experiencing a trial; two, you just got through a trial; or three, you are about to enter a trial. That's how life is.

I don't know what your most recent trial looks like. It could be related to health, finances, your marriage, issues with your boss, relationships with loved ones that are strained, etc. It could be any of these things or about a thousand others. These are all serious, real-life issues we face. But if the stress of these issues overtakes our lives, have we trusted God in our tough situation?

Faith is expensive. It costs us our pride, our sense of control, and sometimes the respect of others who just don't "get it." It simply doesn't make sense to a lot of people when you say, "I have no idea how I'll pay this crazy hospital bill, but I'm trusting God to provide." Say that to some people, and they'll think you've lost it.

But our lives don't look quite like other people's. We are called to hang on to God's every promised word. We are called to walk in victory in the midst of difficult circumstances.

Make no mistake—I get that it's easy for me to write these words, but it's another thing to live them. It requires faith, sacrifice and effort to live out these words. But take a look at Job. God allowed Job to take on some extremely difficult times. Even though he didn't understand how God was working in his life, he remained faithful. Why did God put Job to the test? For the same reason you and I are tested. It allows us to draw closer to Him.

Job's wife told him to curse God and die when he was going through all the pain he endured, but Job didn't listen to his wife's bad advice. He had faith in God his entire life. He remembered how God had previously brought Him through the tough times, and though he wept and mourned and questioned, Job also trusted that God would bring him through his current trials.

I'm alive today because God wanted me to tell you my story. God wanted me to draw closer to Him so that I could hear a message to pass along to you and anyone else I share my story with. What's the message? God wants us to pray more. People prayed for me in true faith, and against all odds and despite all medical reason, I lived.

Sometimes our faith costs us our friends. It did for Job, in a sense. He insisted on holding on to his belief in God's goodness, even when he was suffering terribly, and his wife and friends were horrible comforters. They blamed him for his afflictions and advised him to curse God. When times are tough, do your friends encourage you to draw closer to God? Be prepared because, like Job's friends or wife, some won't. They can't. They don't have faith. They don't have the understanding of who God is because they have never drawn close to Him when times were tough. Instead, they've turned to other things seeking an answer—alcohol, drugs, sex, money, just to name a few. These are the distractions we turn to when we don't believe that God is with us. These things don't help us overcome our problems, of course. They simply mask the pain we experience when we're afflicted.

Truth is, life isn't always fair. And it's not easy to trust God when we're walking through the unfairness of life. It's not easy to endure the hard times, but we must realize God is using all of our circumstances, good and bad, to draw us near to Him. When we get through our crises, they build our testimony of who God is and what He's done for us.

As I write this, nine years after the fact, I am still waiting for full restoration of my lungs and heart. God saved me, but I didn't walk away from my illness unscathed. I have to walk the walk of faith each day, believing that God can heal me completely, and trusting that if He doesn't do it right away, there is purpose in that.

I can't run like I used to. I'm not living the full and complete physical life I was used to living. I still lose my breath at times just walking up a flight of stairs. But I believe God will restore me completely one day. Total healing. That is my hope. Sometimes healing takes time. Not everyone is instantly healed by Jesus. Some are healed along the way. That's my confession. Jesus is healing me along the way for His purpose.

"Being confident of this, that he who began a good work in you will carry it on to completion until the day of Christ Jesus."

—Philippians 1:6

Confidence is difficult. It's difficult to proclaim total deliverance in faith. It's a mind battle to keep your confession and your faith and to remove the seeds of doubt. Satan will try to sow seeds of doubt into your mind, but you can capture those little foxes intent on spoiling the vine. Take authority over those thoughts. Cast them from your mind.

Easier said than done, I know. No one except Jesus has perfect faith, but we can increase our faith by reading His Word. We can increase our faith through prayer and through taking to heart the testimonies of others.

I'm currently facing a situation in my life even harder than what I experienced in the hospital. My second-born daughter, Evelyn Ryanne, was diagnosed with a rare syndrome when she was two months old. After everything I went through with my illness, I bet you're sure I responded with absolute faith, acceptance and peace, right?

Yeah, not exactly. I was devastated. I was angry. I was asking why, begging God to let me switch places with her. Friends, I tell you this to let you know I am not perfect. Yeah, it's true. "Miracle Man" doesn't always have miraculous faith. But my wife and I have committed to laying our little Evelyn at Jesus's feet. Everything we have belongs to God anyway, and that includes our precious children. My girls are my world, but when I lay them at Jesus's feet, the sadness, anger and doubt wash away. I can reclaim my peace and trust and faith that God is working in this situation.

It costs me a lot to commit to trusting God's plan with my baby daughter. It hurts to release control, but He has shown Himself to be faithful in my life in a deeply miraculous way. How am I honoring His faithfulness if I don't trust His plan?

Life isn't easy, and walking in faith isn't easy. But the reward—the peace that surpasses understanding—is so great.

thirteen

Gratitude

During the month I was in the hospital, more than two hundred people came to visit me. People from several states came to my bedside to be with my family. My dad said after I woke from the coma, "I don't know how anyone could make it through life without a church family." Although these hundreds of people came to see me, I didn't know it because I was asleep for most of their visits. But this made a big impact on my family.

We can tell someone we love them, but actions speak louder than words. When we step up and give our time and resources for others, that's love. Love is an action word, not just an emotional expression of feelings in a fleeting moment. Love will motivate us to do selfless things for others, expecting nothing in return but allowing the kindness of Jesus to flow through us.

I owe gratitude to so many people. I hope you'll indulge me for a few minutes while I show some appreciation to those who were instrumental in seeing me and my family through my crisis.

When the doctors told my family I wouldn't live through the night, my parents called my older brother, Daniel. He took the first available flight from Ohio to San Diego late that Sunday night. Daniel is a doctor, and God bless his bosses for understanding the severity of the situation and letting him come home for the whole first week I was in the hospital.

Daniel and I are incredibly close. We're not far apart in age, and for the most part, we have the same interests and hobbies. Except when it comes to studying! I remember coming home several nights in the early hours of the morning, tiptoeing upstairs so my parents wouldn't hear me. He would have his bedroom light on, studying for his med school tests. Maybe you've correctly guessed I was the punk growing up. Daniel would look at me and just shake his head as I walked past his room.

We both love sports, especially baseball, and he is an amazing dad to his kids. Daniel, thank you for being the greatest big brother I could have asked for, and for being here as soon as you could from so far away. I love you more than you know, big bro.

My father, Dan, is self-employed and has owned a custom cabinet business for thirty-plus years. If he doesn't work, the bills do not get paid. That's the reality of being self-employed. There's no sick leave or paid time off. My dad took a ton of time away from work so he could be with my mom and me at the hospital. My little brother, Alex, was about nine years old when I got sick. It was summertime, and there was no school, so my dad took many days off to be with Alex at home, as they did not want him to see me so ill. As my condition improved, he was around a lot more for visits. Alex, seeing your beautiful smile helped me every single day of my recovery! I love you, buddy, and I'm so proud of you! You have a special calling on your life. Seek Jesus always. You are a world-changer.

Thank you, Dad, for sacrificing the business for me. I know you would do it all over again in a second. I know you fell behind with work so much in that month, but God blessed our family and your business immensely after this. You showed the character and integrity of a loving father to all of us during that time, and you did everything you could to keep our family strong. You juggled a business, a marriage, a family, and led them emotionally and spiritually. If I am half the father to my girls that you've been to us, I'll be happy. If I'm half the husband to Lindsay that you've been to Mom, I'll feel like a success. No words can describe the love and appreciation I have for you.

My sister, Sara, and my brother-in-law, Gabe, were so vital during this crisis. As I mentioned before, Gabe and I had a great evening when he was locked in my room one night. Sara was a huge blessing when it came to keeping everyone updated and getting the most accurate news about my condition out to everyone. Sara made sure my mom and dad were well taken care of and provided incredible emotional support to them and my two brothers. Sara and Gabe, I love both of you very much.

Want to know something crazy? This wasn't the first scary, emotional health situation my family had walked through. My mom, Teresa, battled a pretty severe case of breast cancer for quite some time. As you can imagine, it took a toll on our family. It's stressful, to say the least, but rather than tearing us apart, it brought our family closer together. My mom had a mastectomy a month before my hospital stay.

Instead of resting at home, she recovered in the hospital by my bedside. She spent every night in the hospital, with the exception of maybe three or four times. She would sleep in my ICU room, or sometimes in the waiting room. She never complained about her recovery pain. Never. She was totally focused on me.

Later that year, the cancer came back and she had a second mastectomy. But I'm happy to say that, praise God, she is now cancer free!

Once I was released, I lived with my parents for about fourteen months while recovering. I could not drive for several months, and she took me to every doctor appointment. And I was visiting the doctor a lot in those months. Never once did she complain.

I was basically useless. I could barely walk up the stairs, let alone take care of myself or help out around the house. But anytime I needed anything, my mom or someone else in my family was there right away.

Mom, thanks for everything. I can never express the appreciation and love I have for you. I remember one day, you and Dad told me how much it pained you to see me in this condition, not knowing if I would live for the first seven days. Being twenty-four and not being a dad yet, I could not understand the depth of that statement at the time. But I'm a dad now, and I cannot imagine what you guys went through. For parents, being helpless while your children suffer is our worst possible nightmare. I can only imagine how it felt to look at me in that pronation bed, as I lay there lifeless. But with everything out of your control, you guys showed the greatest love by surrendering the situation to Jesus, and praying, praying, and praying some more. Dad, I remember you telling me that you would trade places with me in an instant. I finally understand what you mean. I understand now that whatever hardship my girls face, I would gladly trade places with them in an instant.

I have three best friends, and each one of them was there by my bedside at a moment's notice. Andy, who was my roommate in San Diego when I got sick, lived only a few miles down the road from the hospital, so he was able to be there often. He also was able to take care of our condo situation. Thank you for everything, man. Some of the greatest times of my life are the memories we have made.

Ryan was able to come in from Colorado to see me the first week I was sick. I was in the coma while he was there, so I don't remember his visit. But it meant so much to me, brother, for you to come out and be with my family. You know you are their fourth son!

Daniel, a.k.a. Titus, drove six hours from Phoenix as soon as my mom told him I was on the verge of death. You didn't even think twice about it, did you? I know you and my parents had some long talks while you were out here, and that really helped them through that terrible time. Thank you for being the greatest friend God could ever give me.

Thousands of people prayed for me worldwide. Those who were local made such a huge impact on my family and me. Like I mentioned, more than two hundred people came to visit. I was not awake for most of it, but everyone signed a book. This book was made to write me a note of love and encouragement. I still read through the book often as a reminder of what God did for me, and I am so thankful for every word written in it.

As the majority of the visitors came, they would restock my family with home-cooked meals, water and snacks. In fact, my family had such an abundance of gifts, they always had plenty to share with the other families in the ICU waiting room. Everyone was sharing with one another during this difficult time. The waiting room seriously turned into my parents' home, and during several of those long nights, friends of my family would stay with my mom and dad to keep them company and keep their spirits up. The room was pretty small and it was only big enough to accommodate a blowup mattress, but they made it work!

When my dad said he doesn't know how people can get through life without a church family, he was spot on. I have no clue how people do it. Community is so important.

Some friends would come to the hospital just to visit with my family. Even though I was the one in the coma, the toll it took on my family is unfathomable. They needed the encouragement and support of our friends to help them continue to persevere through the situation. Some would come just to be with my mom because they knew she was recovering from major surgery. Others would come to be with my dad and support him.

I specifically remember one story that was shared with me after I woke up. It is so simple, but to this day, the impact it made will always be appreciated. Two people I really look up to are Doug Balcombe and his wife, Valerie. Pastor Doug was the pastor of the church I grew up in throughout my teenage years. Their son Lance is one of my very close friends, so I spent a lot of time around them in my youth.

Pastor Doug and Valerie were heading out of town, and on the way out, they drove to the hospital. It wasn't to visit me, and it wasn't the longest visit. They were there for maybe ten or fifteen minutes to pray with my mom and dad. They never walked into the room to look at me in the pronation bed. They simply wanted to love on my family and let them know they were not in this situation alone. I never thanked them for that moment, but it has left an imprint in my heart and always will.

This is why it is so important to have community around us.

"Carry each other's burdens, and in this way
you will fulfill the law of Christ."

—*Galatians 6:2*

That is exactly what everyone did for my family. They picked up the heaviness of the situation and were there to encourage and also to weep with them, to lend an ear to listen and a shoulder to cry on. There is no way we can get through life without a community, and a church family is a special kind of community.

One of my mentors, Jeff Brewer, had a job site that was close to the hospital, so he was there twenty-eight out of the thirty days. It was such a breath of fresh air to see his smile. He would bring random food and drinks to surprise me. Some of his visits were long, and some were very short. But every time he came, he would give me a hug, tell me how much he loved me, and pray with me.

My friend Marcus Hillman is possibly the funniest person I know. He is a brother in Christ and just a great guy. He would bring my family coffee and hot chocolate at the most random times. He would show up at 10:30 at night. I would be asleep, but he would visit with them and put some much-needed smiles on their faces. I remember one time in the recovery room, he had me laughing so hard that my heart rate jumped and he had to leave the room. Moments like those helped get me through.

When I got home from the hospital, my immune system was severely weakened. I could not be around people in public for a couple of months. Even going to the grocery store was risky for the first several weeks. A family friend, Alex Najera, lived about forty-five minutes from my parents' house. On Sunday mornings, he would drive up to Ramona and "do church" with me, knowing I could not go to my church.

It wasn't just a one-time thing. Alex came up several times. I would sit on the chair, and he would sit on the couch. He would play guitar and we would worship for a while, and then we'd do a Bible study. I really look up to Alex. He is older than I am and is married with kids. He's the kind of person you can really learn a lot from just by watching him and being around him.

I looked forward to Sundays with Alex. It meant so much to me that he would go out of his way to bless me with church at home when I couldn't leave the house. Those Sundays are moments I will never forget.

I wish I had time to write about every person who impacted my family and me during this time, but it would probably take another book! I wanted to show you all a few examples of community, especially among the people of God, and how it helped us get through.

> *"Two are better than one, because they have a good return for their work: If one falls down, his friend can help him up. But pity the man who falls and has no one to help him up! Also, if two lie down together, they will keep warm. But how can one keep warm alone? Though one may be overpowered, two can defend themselves. A cord of three strands is not quickly broken."*
>
> —*Ecclesiastes 4:9–12*

One of the questions my teen students often ask is, "If someone accepts Christ on their deathbed, are they going to Heaven?"

My reply is that if that person's acceptance is sincere, then yes, they are saved. I believe they will be spending eternity with Jesus. It doesn't matter if you accept Christ at ninety-three in your last days, or age ten with a lifetime ahead of you—you will be living in paradise if you say yes to Jesus. That said, if you accept the Lord in your last days, you miss out on the lifetime of blessings the Lord gives you and the community that He surrounds you with as a believer. Living for Jesus doesn't mean your life will be easier, but it does mean it will be better. One reason it's better is because you have the family of God surrounding you.

My family wouldn't have made it without their church community and their friends. There is no way I would have made it through my recovery without them. Some burdens are just too heavy to bear on our own.

It is so important to have people who can encourage you, love on you, and challenge you. Just as the Word says, iron sharpens iron. We need accountability. We need our friends to remind us when we are slipping and messing up. We need people in our lives who are there for us when we need them.

There is nothing better than having a church family who loves you and cares about you. I love Sundays. I love fellowshipping with my faith community. I pray that you are involved in a supportive church community. I pray you are involved in a life group or other small group Bible study you're able to attend on a weekly basis. I pray that you have a great circle of friends who keep you accountable and will challenge you to grow in your maturity with Christ.

My wife and I are walking through a scary time with our daughter. Her health situation is frightening and stressful. But our family, friends, and church community are walking through this season with us, hand in hand. We are not in this alone. We are surrounded by love and prayers. Life is not easy, but when we are weak, our community is strong. If you're feeling alone in life, I hope this chapter inspires you to seek out a strong faith community who will embrace you, love you and help carry your burdens.

There's a flipside to this, of course. When someone else is in a crisis, we are called to step up and support them. When someone in our community needs us, then we can be the extension of Christ for them. It works both ways. One of the greatest joys in life is being able to comfort those in need, to be an ear for those who need to talk. To just be present in times when someone is feeling alone.

Jesus was near to the weary and the brokenhearted. It's our honor to walk in His example.

fourteen

YOUR STORY

The Friday before I was supposed to be released, one of my doctors walked into my room. He told me he wanted me to remain in the hospital for a couple more days so they could continue to monitor a few things: how my blood clot was, the hole in my neck, my body's reaction to the medication, and so on. Those few days seemed like an eternity to me. I wanted to be out of there so badly, but I trusted God and knew His timing would be better than mine.

But something rad happened early Monday morning before I was sent home.

When I was a senior in Bible college, I had the opportunity to create a course and teach it. Since the calling the Lord put on my life was youth ministry, I created a course called Youth Ministry Survey. Each week, I had a different guest speaker come in and teach us relevant topics that youth pastors need to know, and also discuss topics that are relevant to teens.

It was a really fun class, and the students seemed to enjoy it. I tried to incorporate a variety of speakers. I brought in a gentleman who was a youth pastor for roughly twenty years. I had a former Chargers football player, now marriage counselor, come in. I had a local radio personality come in and speak to the class. His name is Mikey.

Now, I was addicted to his radio show here in San Diego, and it was extremely popular for some time. Mikey is a believer. I'd never met him, but I reached out and asked if he would come bless our class. He graciously accepted, and what an impact he left on all of us that afternoon.

Mikey and I developed a friendship in the years following, and one day, there was a knock on my hospital door, and in walked Mikey. What a welcome surprise! But at first he was confused. "Is this Jonny Rizzo's room?" he asked. He didn't recognize me because the weight loss was so drastic. I didn't look like the same person.

He stayed for quite a while. We had a great visit, and he and my mom talked about her experience having a son at death's door.

And then on the morning of release, Monday, August 24, 2009, I was lying in bed and got a text message from a friend. He said Mikey was talking about H1N1 on his radio show, and he mentioned my name. So I decided to call in. Friends, imagine this: I am on my back with my hospital bed positioned so I can sit up a little bit. I have oxygen in my nose, and I am so weak, I literally cannot hold my phone in my hand. A cell phone weighs maybe seven or eight ounces. That is how weak I had become. I clicked the speakerphone button and laid the phone right under my chin.

For the next fifteen minutes, Mikey interviewed me about my experience. When I answered his questions, I had to place my pointer, middle and ring fingers firmly against the large hole in my neck. Otherwise, no noise would come out when I tried to speak—just a whistling sound. My voice was pretty messed up, but it was strong enough to tell my story— my story of how God brought me through a near-death experience. That testimony was broadcast on the number one radio show in San Diego. Thousands upon thousands of people heard this story on a secular radio station. Amazing!

I didn't hold back. I gave all the glory to God. At one point, I said, "If you do not believe in the power of prayer after hearing my story, you will never believe in it." I was focused and fired up. I was able to tell everyone listening on the radio waves that I was not afraid to die because I had the Lord Jesus Christ as my personal Savior, and that I believed this is why we live—to spend eternity with Christ when we breathe our last breath. I wanted to be sure that all who heard the interview knew who Jesus was after those fifteen minutes.

Before the interview ended, I had already received dozens of text messages, phone calls, emails and direct messages about how powerful it was. But let me be really clear about something; it was *not* about me or my power. I was just sharing the story of what God had done through me. He met me during my illness in such a real, powerful way, it would have been selfish of me to keep that story to myself when I could use it to encourage and bless others.

One of the favorite moments of my life happened shortly after the interview had ended. A couple of hours later, I was still lying in my bed, counting down the hours until I could go home. My mom was busy throughout the room taking down the photos, Bible verses, and signs my friends had made for me to keep a smile on my face. As I was lying there, I heard a quiet knock on the door. The door opened, and in came the sweetest lady dressed in scrubs and hospital gear.

She looked at me and asked in her soft voice, "Are you Mr. Rizzo?"

I made eye contact with her, put three fingers back over my hole, and said, "Yes, I'm him."

This nurse was older, and you could tell she had experienced quite a lot in her career, working in a hospital. She told me that she got in her car that morning, and like she usually does, turned on The Mikey Show to get a quick laugh before she got to work. She heard my interview and heard me say I was at Sharp Grossmont Hospital, which happened to be where she worked.

She told me it was an honor to meet me, but in reality, it was an honor to meet her. She worked across the hospital in the cancer unit. She told me that her job is so hard because she builds relationships with her patients, and the majority of them don't walk out of the hospital the way I was about to. Instead, she has to watch their bodies being wheeled away.

She told me that it had gotten to a point where she couldn't do it anymore because it weighed so heavily on her. But she said my story changed this. The story of God saving my life gave her hope, and on the drive into work when she was going to quit, it gave her a new realization that the kind of work she does is truly making a difference.

She recommitted her mind and heart to continue to be the best nurse she could be for the patients who needed her most. She was a believer, and she knew that if God could heal someone as sick as me, He could heal someone as sick as her cancer patients. But even if He didn't, they still needed her.

She had just seen too many people die, and it took a toll on her. How could it not? As I write these words, I have tears in my eyes. I do not remember her name. I wish I did, but I will always remember her beautiful smile and her kind words.

I don't know if she'll ever read these words, but if she does, I want to thank her for stopping by. That conversation touched my life, and I'll never forget it. Thank you, nurse. I pray you will continue being a blessing to your patients, and I pray you will continue to have hope for the sick.

Mikey's show was the beginning of God using my story to touch others. But it was only the beginning. This unnamed nurse was the first of many people to tell me my story changed them. I've told you about some of the others in earlier chapters.

But do you want to know something? My story isn't the only story able to touch lives. Far, far from it. In fact, *every* story has the potential to touch a life.

Including yours. Friends, share your stories! Every one of you reading this book right now has a story and, even more awesome than that, your story isn't finished yet! Some of you are just in the first couple of pages; others of you are in the final chapters. But no matter where you are in your journey, your story is powerful and it needs to be shared. We need to let others know about what the Lord is doing and has done in our lives.

Don't think for a moment that God can't use you. Don't believe that lie from the enemy.

I think of Paul in the New Testament. He was a murderer of Christians, and he ended up being one of the most important authors in the Bible. He wrote thirteen books. God used him! Look at the life of David; he took someone else's wife, then had that man killed, yet he wrote more than seventy of the psalms. He was an adulterer and murderer, but he turned to the Lord, and God used him. God can and wants to use you for His glory, and we glorify Him by sharing our stories of what God is doing in and through us.

Sometimes we get the idea that the best testimonies are flashy ones—the ones where someone had been homeless, in a gang, a murderer, a drug addict, and now they are living life for Jesus. Don't get me wrong—those stories are very powerful, but do you know what else is powerful? The person who gives his life to Jesus at a young age and is able to say no to the offerings of this world—someone who doesn't touch drugs and stays sexually pure for their spouse on their wedding night. That's a powerful story too.

No matter what your story is, you have something to share that will bless someone who needs to hear it. Don't be selfish and hold it in. We must open up our mouths and talk. Your story can reach some mine can't, and vice versa.

People are desperate to find hope in this life. People are running to anything they think will give them happiness, but they are turning to the wrong things. Possessions, money, sex, drugs, unhealthy relationships—all of these will leave us empty. Hurting. The only thing—and I mean the *only* thing—that can fill that void is a relationship with Jesus Christ. So many people are searching, and if we are not doing our part by sharing our testimonies, then we need to start now. They are searching for what we have.

Want to know how powerful it can be when you share stories? Check this out.

I told you I never wanted to go to Asia, but God sent me three times, and now the people of China and Japan are always on my heart.

Before my first trip to China, my team met twice a week for six months to prepare. Mostly we prayed. The theme of this trip was "Going After the One." The goal was to make a difference, even if that difference was in one person's life. Every team member prayed for their "one." We didn't know who it would be, of course, but we prayed God would give us the chance to show Jesus to the one person He wanted us to.

One night in China, we were hanging out with the students on their university campus, and there was a young lady sitting by herself on the curb. I approached her and asked if I could sit and talk to her. She said yes, and we talked for a good half-hour. Her name was Bird, and she spoke English really well, so there was no language barrier. We talked about everything, including her goals, her family and her life. She asked about mine and after a few minutes of talking, she asked me about Jesus.

Now, this missions trip was before I got sick, but I had seen the Lord move like crazy in my life and I was fired up to tell everyone about Jesus. My testimony was not as incredible as it is now, but it was still pretty awesome. Remember, all stories are powerful, not just the flashy ones.

I shared with her about Jesus—how He loves her, how He died on the cross for her sins. I told her about my relationship with Jesus, and how my life had completely changed when I started to live for Him and not myself. She was afraid that if she served the Lord, her family would never talk to her again. Then she hurriedly changed the subject and the conversation wrapped up pretty quickly after that.

As I was walking away from Bird, I was actually pretty frustrated. Who was my one? Who was this person I had been praying for over the last several months? We had been in China for a few days, and I still had not met my one.

In that moment, God spoke clearly to me: "Bird. That is your one. Go back and talk to her again."

I couldn't believe it. It couldn't be Bird. I had tried for half an hour to share the Gospel with her, and it was going nowhere. She was too afraid.

But I turned around, and there she was, still sitting on the curb by herself. I walked back to her, sat down, and almost before my behind hit the curb, she said, "I want that Jesus that you have." Praise God!

I put my arm around her, we prayed, and she accepted the Lord into her life. From that moment on, her life was changed.

Guess what happened?

The next year, we went back to China. We had built a relationship with the university, so we went back to see our friends there. We were a few days into the trip, and I had seen several people we'd met the previous year, but not Bird. I had been looking forward to seeing her and was pretty bummed that she didn't seem to be there.

Our group of twelve packed up early one morning, hopped on a bus, and drove to a cave. It was a huge cave—it was one of the most beautiful things I have ever seen. It went a couple of miles in, and there was a river that flowed through it. Just spectacular. But it was a long, hot day. At the end of it, I was exhausted, very sweaty, and ready to get back to our hotel room.

So I wasn't thrilled when our bus stopped on a road close to our hotel and three of my friends told me we were going somewhere—somewhere besides the hotel room with its warm showers and cool air conditioning. Normally, I'm up for adventuring, but this time, all I wanted was that hotel room. So I was angry and grumbling as we walked down a dirt road for four or five blocks.

We arrived at a house that was nothing out of the ordinary, and the missionary with us led us up the front steps. At the top of the stairs was an open room. It wasn't big, but there were at least fifty people crammed in there. A single ceiling fan pushed the hot air around the room. But that didn't stop the people inside from lifting their hands and singing their hearts out to the King of Kings.

My bad attitude melted away. I realized I was standing in an underground Chinese church. We stayed for close to four hours that night, fellowshipping and worshipping with our brothers and sisters in Christ who lived all the way across the globe.

I sat in a chair next to one of my friends, but a few chairs down, a young woman sat. She looked familiar. Then it dawned on me—it was Bird! It was my one! The one who, a year prior, I had been praying for and whom I had led to Christ. Once we recognized each other, we jumped up and hugged. I couldn't believe it. What were the odds?

Let me tell you what happened to Bird. God moved mightily in her heart after she gave her life to Him. Bird was so on fire for the Lord, she started a Bible study on the campus of her secular university of roughly fourteen thousand students. Young people were giving their lives to Christ left and right, and it was all because of Bird's passion to reach the unsaved.

Bird shared her story with everyone. She told everyone about how Christ had changed her life. She was the one in charge of these underground church meetings. I was so in awe that when I gave her that hug, I had tears rolling down my face. I thanked Jesus for allowing me to see her again, and to see the ministry she had started on her campus in the midst of a godless environment.

One person. She was my one person. And then she found one person. And another and another. The story of who Jesus was to me, shared with Bird, rippled outward to many people.

Friends, please understand this isn't about me and it isn't about Bird. It's about the way God used our stories to touch many lives.

You are unique. There is no one else like you. How rad is that? No matter where you are in life right now, you have a story that needs to be heard. You may have had marriage issues, and God renewed that relationship. Go encourage a couple who is going through what you once endured. You may have had financial issues, and the Lord had His provision over you. Go share with someone who is struggling with finances, and encourage them to give it over to the Lord. The examples are endless.

Share what the Lord is doing through you. You are important, and so is your story.

There is nothing to be ashamed of when we are washed clean by the blood of Christ. We are not perfect. We all sin, but He uses every situation for good.

So please don't hold in your story. You never know how it could impact someone. When I spoke to Bird, I was in my early twenties, in a faraway country, having a conversation with some random stranger, just sharing about the love Jesus has for all of us. I am so glad God gave me the boldness and courage to share at that moment.

There have been many times when I had the opportunity to share with people, and I wasn't bold. I was embarrassed, or people were watching me, so I felt uncomfortable. It happens. But I always pray for boldness now. Time is short. We have to take advantage of the opportunities we're given.

There are some parts of the story about my illness that are unsavory, but I have no problem being very open now about what I went through in the hospital. That experience helped shape me into who I am today. That story has power. *Your* story has power. Bless others with it, because it does need to be out there. You're the only person who can share your story. So the question is, will you?

FINAL THOUGHTS

I never thought I would write a book, and I certainly don't know if I will ever write another one. So while I am at it, I just wanted to write up some thoughts I have—little snippets about what God has been doing in my life—and share them with you. I hope what you are about to read encourages you. Some of these thoughts are related to what we've been talking about in this book, and others are not. But they are just my real, raw thoughts, and I hope you enjoy them.

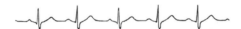

I've been part of the church my entire life. I grew up there. I loved going to church on Sunday mornings, and it was always something that we did as a family. It was nonnegotiable. Sunday was church and family day, and we all loved it. I always had a real relationship with Jesus, and I always knew who God was and what the Bible said, for the most part. Growing up, I always had morals, and knew there were certain things I just wouldn't partake in, no matter what.

Or so I thought.

When I was eighteen years old, I was going through a tough time in my life. I had made some dumb decisions and was at a crossroads in my life. I was fresh out of high school, immature, and unclear what college I would be going to, if I was even going to go at all. Even though I knew who God was, I was not really walking with Him at that time. I struggled a lot.

One day, I was driving down the road, and God gave me the most incredible vision. He spoke to me. Now, when you are not walking with the Lord and He suddenly speaks to you, you *know* it is Him! It was very, very clear. In this vision, I was at the local stadium here in San Diego, which holds roughly sixty-five thousand seats. The entire stadium was packed, and there was a red carpet that went from the parking lot, onto the field, and stopped at the podium, which is where second base would be. I walked out and stood at that podium. I was the guest speaker that night, giving my testimony.

It freaked me out, but it was so real.

I never told anybody about this vision. I wasn't really sure what it meant.

Three years later, when I was twenty-one, I still knew who God was, but I was beginning to waver in my faith. I had one foot in and one foot out, if you will. I was caught up in the fleshly desires that the world offers. I was not living the life I knew I should. I wasn't walking in the morals I had been raised with. It was definitely a rough place to be.

And then, it happened again. I remember it like it was yesterday. This exact same vision showed up, and again, God spoke to me. Again, when you aren't exactly living your life for Jesus, and He shows up like this, it's very obvious that it's Him speaking and not your own thoughts. In those low valleys, your thoughts tend to be pretty far from God.

It was the same vision. The same stadium, the same sixty-five thousand seats with sixty-five thousand people in them, the same red carpet, and the same podium in the middle of the infield where second base is. I walked out, and I shared my testimony of what God has done in my life.

Even after this second time, I never told anyone.

I mentioned in the earlier chapters that my mother spent all but a few nights sleeping either in my hospital room beside my bed or in the waiting room. Just a handful of nights she left to get a real night's sleep. One of those days she needed to just get away and get some "time off," so she drove home to shower and get fresh clothes.

She later told me in the recovery room one day when we were sitting there, just the two of us, about one of these nights at home. She said the day she went home to shower, she was leaning over the tub shaving one of her legs, and God gave her the clearest and most beautiful vision. This vision came when I was at my most critical, when the doctors didn't know if I would live or die. In this vision, I was standing on red carpet, in a stadium, speaking in front of thousands of people.

When she told me this in the hospital, I started to cry. I was so emotional. I never told her, or anyone for that matter, about the two visions I had, but I shared them with her then. The vision God gave her about me was the same vision God had given me back when I wasn't walking closely with Him.

God is so good. What He showed me was confirmed through her. I don't exactly know what these visions mean. I don't know if that's a literal event that will happen someday. I have never been invited to speak in front of groups of more than a few hundred people. But what I do know is that the good Lord is going to continue to use me, just as He is going to use you, as long as you allow Him to.

I do think it's possible that one day I will be speaking in a stadium in front of sixty-five thousand people, sharing with them the amazing healing God performed in my life. I also believe the day that it happens, people will give their lives to Christ or renew their relationship with Him.

I remember one night I was alone in the hospital a couple of days after waking up from the coma. I was still in the ICU, and I was an absolute mess. It was late at night, and I was starting to finally come to an understanding of what was happening. I was so angry, so bitter.

Why hadn't God just allowed me to die? Even though I was alive, I knew the uphill battle I was facing, and in that moment, dying seemed better than facing reality. In that moment, I wished I were dead. I was broken. I was done. I didn't understand.

I buzzed the night nurse, and when she came in, I motioned to her to play some worship music. As the music played, my room filled with a sense of hope and peace. I felt the Lord's presence come upon me. I just started to cry my eyes out. I was alone, but I knew God was with me.

My body was so weak. Man, was I weak. But as I lay in my bed with so many lines hooked up to my incredibly thin frame, I collected every ounce of energy and strength within me and lifted my arms to worship my King. I cried out to God, and to this day, I still do not know how I was able to lift up my arms, but I did. I surrendered to Jesus. I realized right then and there that the reason I was alive was because my work here on earth was far from finished. That moment is when I knew I would be okay, and I would work my hardest to get back to living a normal life, with the help of Christ.

This reminds me of Exodus 17, which happens to be one of my favorite chapters in the entire Bible. In this chapter, we see such a powerful story of Moses leaning on God. The Amalekites were attacking the Israelites. Moses ordered Joshua to go and fight the Amalekites, and Moses, Aaron, and Hur went to the top of the hill. When Moses had his arms raised, the Israelites would win the battle, and whenever Moses lowered his hands, the Amalekites would win.

Moses's arms got tired, so Aaron and Hur got a stone and sat Moses down on it. Then one of the greatest parts of this story happened: Aaron took one arm, and Hur took the other, and they held Moses's hands up in the air. The Bible says that Moses's hands remained steady until sunset. How amazing is this story?!

Joshua and his army down below were able to defeat the Amalekite army because Moses was able to keep his hands lifted.

Raising your hands to the Lord means many things. One of the things it means to me is surrendering. We cannot do this life on our own. We need the help of God to get us through. Isn't it awesome that Joshua was winning when Moses's hands were raised!

When I was in that hospital room and raised my hands in worship, I was winning. I surrendered my situation to Him. When we draw near to the Lord, we win.

Another thing that is important to notice here is the relationship between Aaron and Hur. Aaron and Moses were brothers, and Hur was a friend. This is the type of friendship we need. We need to surround ourselves with people who will be there with us when we are mentally, physically, and spiritually weak. When we face battles of any kind—health issues, marriage issues, financial issues, whatever it is—we need to turn to a friend we can lean on. They can hold up our hands when we get tired, and we have the honor of doing the same for them in their times of need.

When I lifted my hands to the Lord that night, I won. Even in the most intense of circumstances, we win when we surrender to the Lord. When I was in the hospital—and still today—I am so amazingly blessed to have incredible family and friends who hold me up when I am down. They are my Aaron and Hur. Who are the Aarons and Hurs in your life? Thank God for them because they are tremendous blessings.

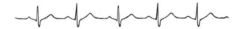

When I met with Pastor Dennis in my hospital room and told him about my experience in Heaven, I was so nervous. But it was Dennis who encouraged me to share this story. He believed every word, no matter how incredible it sounded. It got me thinking. Before my hospital stay, I had read a couple of books. One was about someone who died in a car accident, went to Heaven, and came back to life and wrote about it. The other was about someone who was sent to Hell for several minutes and came back to share his experience. Both were super wild, and neither had happened to me at the time I read these stories.

When I read those books, I thought one of two things had to be true. One: these authors were completely authentic and honest, and these things really happened to them. Or two: they made it all up just to make a buck and get some fame.

As I was reading, I chose to believe those authors. I reasoned that just because it had never happened to me, it didn't mean those experiences never happened to anyone. God uses different people for different situations. How foolish would it be for me to say something wasn't real because I had never experienced it?

I also figured that if those people were lying and using false testimonies to gain fame and fortune, God would deal with them.

When I wrote this book, I knew there would be doubters, and that's okay. There is nothing I can do about that. I understand that some parts of my story are beyond belief, but as I mentioned previously, I wrote this book out of obedience. God told me to share my story, and that's what I am doing.

God uses each person differently. All I ask of the people who hear this testimony, whether through these pages or elsewhere, is to please have an open mind and heart. Read these words, and pay attention to whether God is touching your heart through them. If you're reading this book right now, I believe it's because God wants to use it to touch you in some way.

Jesus loves *you* so much that He died on the cross for *you*. How awesome is that! Isn't it cool to know that if you were the only person on earth, He still would have died for you? That is the depth of love He has. That is unconditional love. God's love for us doesn't change or waver.

It is completely different than what we think love is here on earth. When Jesus died that brutal death on the cross, that was the ultimate sacrifice. He was dead for three days, and then rose and is actively alive and wants to live in your heart. His blood covers all sin. This is a free gift that everyone has access to. To live my life for Jesus has been the greatest decision I have ever made.

Living a life for Christ doesn't mean life will be easier; it means it will be better. There is nothing bigger than God. No problem is too big, no obstacle that He can't conquer. I have tried to live life on my own. You may have tried too, or maybe that's where you're at right now. You may feel like you're just spinning your tires and not getting anywhere.

Trust me, I get it. I have been there. It wasn't until I fully surrendered my life to Christ that I really did experience true freedom; true peace, joy and love. I found my identity was in Christ. It used to be in worldly things: sex, money, popularity, the clothes I wore—the list goes on and on.

When I fully surrendered to Christ, my view of people changed, and my view of myself changed. I realized that I was created for a reason, for a purpose. This purpose is so much more than I could ever have dreamed or written about.

You are created for a purpose, also. God wants the best for you. He wants you to stop doing life on your own with your own agenda. He wants you to surrender to Him, to give one hundred percent to Him.

"He must become greater; I must become less."

—John 3:30

In other words, we need to decrease, so that He can increase in us.

You see, we all have greatness in us. We are all created to do amazing things, beyond anything you or I could ever imagine! But, in order for us to find the true value and purpose of why we were created, we must turn to the Creator. If we never turn our eyes, heart, mind, and focus to Christ, we just won't get it. We won't understand the true reason why we are here.

No matter what you have been told, you are not a mistake. You are not a failure. God took His time with you. He knew you before you were even born. How awesome is that? God cares about you so much that He knows each hair on your head. He longs to have a relationship with each of us. Please do not miss out. No matter what you are going through, do not give up. Stay the course. Seek Jesus, and your life will never be the same.

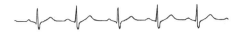

Jesus was thirty-three years old when He died on the cross and shed His blood so we will not die to our sin. While on earth, Jesus performed thousands upon thousands of miracles. The Bible says that if everything Jesus did was written down, there would basically be no room for all of the stories. He made the blind see, the deaf hear, the dead rise, the sick healed, and on and on.

> *"I tell you the truth, anyone who has faith in me will do what I have been doing. He will do even greater things than these, because I am going to the Father."*
>
> —*John 14:12*

These are words straight from Jesus Himself! How awesome is this? Jesus gives us the authority, through the Holy Spirit, to go around and do what He had been doing while walking the Earth. Not only that, but we have the ability to do even greater things. This is so exciting!

Do you believe this? Do you truly, fully believe that we have the gifts necessary to be the hands and feet of Christ?

Some things that may hold us back are fear, not fully believing, or making the excuse that because we haven't seen it, it can't be done. But the promise is right there. We are able to, when we walk with the Holy

Spirit. We cannot do this with our own talent, skills or ability. We must have faith in Jesus.

If this is a spot where you are lacking, just pray. Pray for God to show you the way and He will. Pray for boldness for when the opportunities present themselves to us. If we have a heavenly mindset, our eyes and hearts will be open to see clearly.

One thing we always have to remember: We cannot allow our circumstance to dictate our faith.

God bless you.

If you prayed that prayer and accepted Christ into your heart as your Lord and Savior when you were reading Chapter 10, please send an email and let us know so we can pray for you and support you in your walk.

threehourstolive@gmail.com

AFTERWORD

by Wade LeBlanc, MLB Player

In one of the most humble and energetic stories you will ever read, Jonathan opens his heart and his life to his readers and begs us to turn to Jesus. If we have already done so, he pleads with us to commit our lives to helping others do the same. Many people have published similar stories of meeting Jesus, who reveals a glimpse of Heaven, then turns and also gives the writer a glimpse of Hell. Understandably, if only because we as humans cannot possibly begin to imagine the scenes that were laid out before these individuals, questions and uncertainties will always be raised. However, to know this man and to know his love for the Son of Man, is to know that you are walking through the most uncertain time of Jonathan's life, step by step alongside him, and that every word of his story is true and every ounce of his passion is real.

Jonathan's personal story through the valley of death, back to life, and the earthly struggles that followed, is a harrowing journey through the unknown, even down to exactly what was causing his health to fail him. One of the countless beauties of God, however, is that He will *always* make known that which was unknown. The key here being that it can only happen in His perfect time. One thing Jonathan is proof of is that out of the unknown will always come a platform from which we can show the world the glory of God. What comes with each platform is a calling from God, and it becomes our responsibility, as His chosen children, to answer these callings with humility and passion for the truth.

One thing Jonathan mentions several times throughout this book is that we all have a testimony. This is something that I gain more appreciation for as time goes by. Whether you have gone through a life-changing event that left God as your only hope, or you have been raised in faith and have never strayed, there is a testimony in every circumstance. As Jonathan mentions, the devil will try to convince you that your story isn't worth telling. God, on the other hand, assures us otherwise.

There are two sides to every story—on one side is the devil telling you your story is irrelevant. On the other? Your personal experiences with God that nobody can take away. In *Three Hours to Live*, Jonathan has laid out his truth for the world to read. As my brother-in-law, and spiritual advisor, Nick Perioux once asked, "Who is telling your truth?"

ACKNOWLEDGMENTS

I would like to thank my family—my father, Dan, my mother, Teresa, Sara, Daniel, Alex, and Gabe. Thank you for all the sacrifices you have made. I love you guys.

To my very pregnant wife, Lindsay, and our daughters, Cecelia and Evelyn. Thank you for supporting me in this project, and for understanding all the late nights and meetings. I love you girls.

Thank you to all the churches that had me speak, the friends who visited, and the prayer warriors near and far who were on their knees praying for me.

Thank you to all the doctors, nurses, hospital staff, and everyone at Sharp Grossmont Hospital. You are the best!

Thank you to Lindsay Franklin for being my mentor throughout this process, and for sharing the same vision I do. There is no greater editor than you.

Thank you to "Coach" Pete Zindler for giving me the vision to get my story out, and for encouraging me to be obedient to the Lord. You are a huge part of why this book came to be.

jonathan rizzo

ABOUT THE AUTHOR

Jonathan Rizzo is a youth pastor in the Ocean Beach area of San Diego, where he lives with his wife and their three beautiful daughters. Jonathan is a lifelong follower of Christ, and he travels the world to share about his near-death experience as a young man—to turn his nightmare into a source of encouragement and light for others. When he's not spending time with his family, he's living and breathing baseball, working out in the gym, or rocking out on the drums.

To contact Jonathan for prayer requests, speaking engagements, or any other inquiries, please visit

www.jonathanrizzo.org

Or contact via email
threehourstolive@gmail.com

To support The Rory Graham Jr. Foundation, please visit

www.rorygrahamjr.org

Or contact via email
help@rorygrahamjr.org